Canadian Living's

FAMILY
COOKBOOK

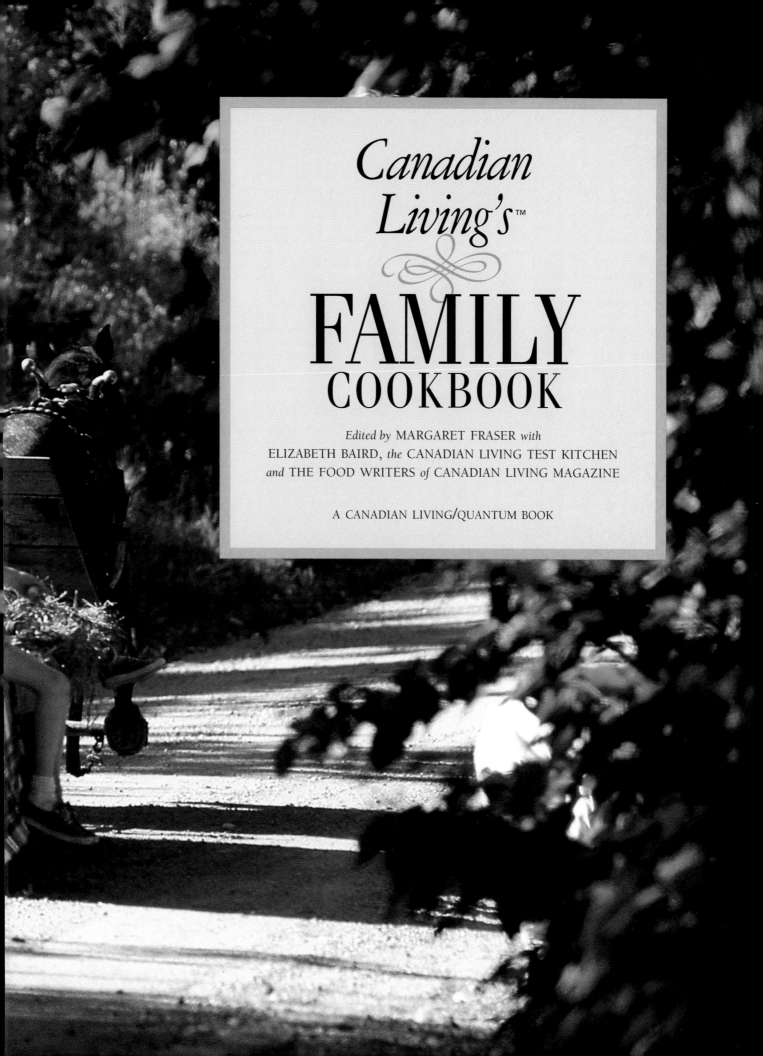

Canadian Living's

FAMILY
COOKBOOK

Edited by MARGARET FRASER *with*
ELIZABETH BAIRD, *the* CANADIAN LIVING TEST KITCHEN
and THE FOOD WRITERS *of* CANADIAN LIVING MAGAZINE

A CANADIAN LIVING/QUANTUM BOOK

Canadian Cataloguing in Publication Data

Fraser, Margaret

Canadian Living's family cookbook

"A Canadian Living/Quantum Book."

Issued also in French under title:
Coup de pouce Tout le monde à table.

Includes index.
ISBN 1-895892-04-X

1. Cookery.   I. Title   II. Title: Family cookbook.

TX714.F73 1995   641.5   C95-930564-5

**Produced by Madison Press Books
for The Quantum Book Group Inc.
149 Lowther Avenue, Toronto, Ontario, Canada M5R 3M5**

Printed in Canada

CONTENTS

Cinnamon Ice Cream (p. 174)   *Christmas Tea (p. 178)*

A Family Reunion (p. 110)   *Crunchy Lobster Rolls (p. 122)*

One-Bowl Birthday Cake (p. 34)

*(above) The Little Hatters'
Tea Party (p. 48); (below)
Harvest Pumpkin Pie
(p. 138)*

FOR ALL THE GOOD TIMES!

Food and families just naturally go together. Few things in life are more rewarding than friends and family gathering for a satisfying, delicious meal. At *Canadian Living* our families speak many languages and celebrate a variety of special occasions. They come in all shapes and sizes and include everyone from toddlers and teenagers to singles and empty nesters.

That's why this unique new cookbook presents a tempting selection of recipes and menus for all kinds of occasions, from those relaxing weekends when it's fun to cook something special to great ideas for perking up busy weeknight suppers. There are recipes for the special days we all celebrate — birthdays, weddings, anniversaries and reunions — as well as for all the holidays and traditional celebrations that mark the calendar and the seasons of the Canadian year.

If you want to make this Halloween extra spooky, for example, we have terrific house-haunting suggestions, witch's fingers to crunch on and new ideas for candy apples. Our Thanksgiving dinner is a festive meal with a difference, and we have 32 pages of everything you need to make the Christmas season a delight.

You can easily mix and match recipes from different chapters to create your own style of cooking for lunches, brunches and potluck get-togethers. Choose some make-ahead dishes to stock the freezer or meatless dishes for vegetarians. There's even a chapter of recipes that kids can cook themselves with the kinds of food they love to eat. And as with all *Canadian Living* books, our recipes are tested-till-perfect for success in your kitchen every time.

We're sure that as you browse through the colorful pages of our new *Family Cookbook*, you'll find yourself planning the kinds of occasions that memories are made of.

— Elizabeth Baird
Food Director, *Canadian Living* Magazine

Chapter One

The WEEKEND IS SPECIAL

Everyone loves the weekend.
Entertain family and friends with a
savory meal or offer an array of tempting
appetizers when the gang drops in.
For a lazy Saturday, there's even
make-aheads to have stashed in the freezer.

Chicken with Sage, Tomatoes and Lemon

Simple enough for rush-hour suppers, yet impressive enough for company, this is Italian-style country cooking at its best. Serve with fluffy rice and lightly sautéed zucchini.

4	chicken breasts	4
3 tbsp	olive oil	50 mL
3/4 tsp	salt	4 mL
1/2 tsp	pepper	2 mL
1	onion, chopped	1
2	cloves garlic, minced	2
1	large carrot, chopped	1
1 tbsp	finely grated lemon rind	15 mL
1 tbsp	chopped fresh sage (or 1 tsp/5 mL dried)	15 mL
1	large tomato, peeled, seeded and chopped	1
1/3 cup	chicken stock	75 mL
3 tbsp	lemon juice	50 mL
	Fresh sage leaves	
	Lemon slices	

Remove skin from chicken; debone if desired. In large skillet, heat oil over medium heat; cook chicken and pinch each of the salt and pepper, turning once, for 5 to 7 minutes or until lightly browned. Remove to plate; cover and keep warm.

ᖺ Add onion, garlic and carrot to pan; cook, stirring often, for about 5 minutes or until onion starts to turn golden. Stir in lemon rind, sage and remaining salt and pepper; cook for 1 minute.

ᖺ Add tomato and chicken stock, stirring to scrape up brown bits; bring to boil. Reduce heat and return chicken to pan; cover and simmer for 15 minutes, turning chicken once.

ᖺ Stir in lemon juice; cook, uncovered, for 5 to 10 minutes or until chicken is no longer pink inside. Serve with pan juices. Garnish with sage leaves and lemon slices. Makes 4 servings.

Stuffed Sherried Chicken Breasts

Light yet full of flavor, these make-ahead chicken breasts beg to be shared with good friends.

6	boneless skinless chicken breasts (1-1/2 lb/750 g)	6
1 tsp	butter	5 mL
1/2 cup	dry sherry	125 mL
	STUFFING	
12	large spinach leaves	12
1 tbsp	butter	15 mL
1	onion, chopped	1
2	cloves garlic, minced	2
1 cup	coarsely grated zucchini	250 mL
1/2 cup	coarsely grated carrot	125 mL
1/2 tsp	dried thyme	2 mL
1/2 cup	fresh bread crumbs	125 mL
2 tbsp	chopped fresh parsley	25 mL
1	egg white	1
1/4 tsp	each salt and pepper	1 mL

Between sheets of waxed paper, pound chicken to 1/4-inch (5 mm) thickness.

STUFFING: Trim spinach and rinse under water; shake off excess water. In saucepan, cover spinach and cook over medium-high heat, with just the water clinging to leaves, for 1 minute or until just wilted; drain and set aside.

In nonstick skillet, melt 1 tbsp (15 mL) butter over medium heat; cook onion and garlic for 3 minutes or until softened. Stir in zucchini, carrot and thyme; cook, stirring often, for 5 minutes or until tender. Remove from heat. Add bread crumbs, parsley, egg white, salt and pepper; mix well.

Top each chicken breast with 2 spinach leaves; spread stuffing evenly over spinach. Carefully roll up each breast and tie each end with cotton string. *(Chicken can be prepared to this point, covered and refrigerated for up to 8 hours.)*

In large nonstick skillet, melt butter over medium heat; cook stuffed breasts, turning occasionally, for 5 minutes. Pour in sherry; reduce heat to medium-low and cook, covered, for 10 to 12 minutes or until chicken is no longer pink inside, turning to coat in sauce for last 2 minutes. Let stand for 5 minutes. Untie each roll and cut diagonally into 3 or 4 slices. Makes 6 servings.

Spicy Lamb Moussaka

A classic Middle Eastern dish, moussaka is eggplant layered with fragrant lamb and Parmesan-laced sauces. Take it to the cottage or freeze for emergency entertaining. Serve with crusty rolls and mixed greens.

1	eggplant (about 1 lb/500 g)	1
1 tbsp	salt	15 mL
1 tbsp	dry bread crumbs	15 mL
	MEAT SAUCE	
1 lb	ground lamb	500 g
1	onion, chopped	1
1	can (5-1/2 oz/156 mL) tomato paste	1
1/2 cup	dry red wine or beef stock	125 mL
1 tsp	cinnamon	5 mL
1/2 tsp	dried oregano	2 mL
1/4 tsp	each salt and pepper	1 mL
	WHITE SAUCE	
2 tbsp	butter	25 mL
2 tbsp	all-purpose flour	25 mL
1/4 tsp	ground nutmeg	1 mL
Pinch	each salt and pepper	Pinch
1 cup	milk	250 mL
1	egg, lightly beaten	1
2 tbsp	freshly grated Parmesan cheese	25 mL

Cut eggplant crosswise into 1/2-inch (1 cm) thick slices. Place in colander and sprinkle with salt; let stand to drain for 20 minutes. Rinse under cold water; drain on paper towels and pat dry. In saucepan of boiling water, cook eggplant for 3 minutes; drain well.

❧ MEAT SAUCE: In large skillet, cook lamb and onion over medium heat, breaking up meat with back of spoon, until meat is no longer pink. Drain off fat. Stir in tomato paste, wine, cinnamon, oregano, salt and pepper; bring to boil. Reduce heat and simmer for 5 minutes; set aside.

TIP: Substitute ground beef for lamb if you prefer.

❧ WHITE SAUCE: In saucepan, melt butter over medium heat; stir in flour and cook, stirring, for 1 minute. Season with nutmeg, salt and pepper. Gradually whisk in milk until smooth; cook, stirring constantly, for 5 minutes or until thickened slightly.

❧ Stir a little of the hot sauce into egg; return to saucepan and cook, stirring, for about 1 minute or until thickened. Remove from heat; stir in Parmesan until melted.

❧ Sprinkle lightly greased 8-cup (2 L) freezer-to-oven casserole with bread crumbs. Arrange half of the eggplant over bottom; top with meat sauce. Cover with remaining eggplant; pour white sauce over top. (*Moussaka can be prepared to this point, cooled in refrigerator, wrapped well and frozen for up to 3 months; bake frozen moussaka, uncovered, in 375°F/190°C oven for 1 hour and 15 minutes or until bubbly.*)

❧ Bake moussaka, uncovered, in 375°F (190°C) oven for 30 to 40 minutes or until bubbly. Makes about 4 servings.

WHEN YOUR MENU CALLS FOR "MIXED GREENS"

Often just adding a green salad with a light Classic Vinaigrette (recipe follows) is enough to round out a meal. Choose your favorite greens as the base — spinach, romaine, iceberg or Bibb lettuce. Add a contrasting color or flavor, such as dark radicchio, peppery arugula, sharp Belgian endive or simple watercress.

❧ *Add the crunch of toasted nuts, diced unpeeled apple or pear, sprouts (bean or radish), croutons, celery or cucumber slices.*

❧ *Change the salad with toppings such as grated Parmesan, tomato wedges, Spanish or red onion rings, or thinly sliced mushrooms.*

❧ *Toss with a Classic Vinaigrette: Whisk together 1/4 cup (50 mL)*

wine vinegar, 1 tsp (5 mL) each Dijon mustard and liquid honey, salt and pepper to taste, and 1 clove garlic, minced. Gradually whisk in 2/3 cup (150 mL) vegetable oil. Add 1 tbsp (15 mL) chopped fresh herbs if desired — tarragon, parsley or chives. Keep dressing in the refrigerator. Makes about 3/4 cup (175 mL).

Grilled Lamb Shanks

These tasty lamb shanks are scrumptious, especially when braised
then grilled over a hot fire. The braising juice becomes a sauce to serve with pasta or mashed potatoes.
Toss a crisp green salad to go alongside.

2 tbsp	olive oil	25 mL
4	lamb shanks (about 3 lb/1.5 kg)	4
1	carrot, diced	1
1	onion, chopped	1
12	cloves garlic	12
2-1/2 cups	beef stock	625 mL
1/4 cup	chopped fresh parsley	50 mL
1/2 tsp	dried thyme	2 mL
1	bay leaf	1
	Salt and pepper	

In large Dutch oven, heat oil over medium-high heat; brown shanks on all sides, 8 to 10 minutes. Remove from pan and set aside.

Reduce heat to medium; cook carrot, onion and garlic for 5 minutes, stirring often. Stir in 2 cups (500 mL) of the stock, parsley, thyme, bay leaf, and salt and pepper to taste; bring to boil.

Return shanks to pan; cover and cook in 325°F (160°C) oven for 2-1/2 hours, turning meat occasionally. (*Lamb can be prepared to this point, covered and cooled in refrigerator and stored for up to 1 day. Let stand at room temperature for 30 minutes.*)

Reserving liquid, place lamb on greased grill over medium-high heat; cook for 10 to 15 minutes or until browned all over.

Meanwhile, remove bay leaf and skim off fat from liquid. Pour liquid and vegetables into blender or food processor; purée, thinning with remaining beef stock if desired. Serve with lamb. Makes 4 servings.

Mellow Pot Roast with Onions

When family and friends are expected for dinner,
fill the house with the heady aroma of a pot roast slowly baking in the oven.

3 cups	thinly sliced onions	750 mL
3	cloves garlic, minced	3
1	lean boneless short rib roast (about 3 lb/1.5 kg)	1
	Pepper	
1 tbsp	cornstarch	15 mL

Arrange half of the onions and garlic over bottom of Dutch oven. Place roast on top. Cover with remaining onions and garlic. Sprinkle with pepper to taste. Pour in 1/4 cup (50 mL) water.

Cover and roast in 325°F (160°C) oven for 2-1/2 to 3 hours or until meat is tender. Transfer meat and onions to serving platter.

Skim off fat from liquid in pan; add enough water, if necessary, to make 1 cup (250 mL). Dissolve cornstarch in 1 tbsp (15 mL) cold water; add to pan and cook, stirring, for 2 to 3 minutes or until boiling and thickened. Serve with pot roast. Makes 6 to 8 servings.

Meatball and Penne Casserole

*This easy-to-prepare dish is a great make-ahead for a crowd. Penne, the straight tubular noodle,
is available at most supermarkets, but any noodle or macaroni can be used.*

4 cups	penne noodles (about 3/4 lb/375 g)	1 L
1	egg	1
2 lb	ground beef	1 kg
1 cup	fresh bread crumbs	250 mL
2 tsp	dried thyme (or 2 tbsp/25 mL chopped fresh)	10 mL
1 tbsp	vegetable oil	15 mL
1	large onion, chopped	1
1 cup	chopped green onions	250 mL
4	cloves garlic, minced	4
1	sweet green or red pepper, coarsely chopped	1
3 cups	sliced mushrooms (about 1/2 lb/250 g)	750 mL
2 cups	sliced celery	500 mL
1 tsp	each dried oregano and basil	5 mL
2	cans (each 14 oz/398 mL) tomato sauce	2
1/2 cup	chopped fresh parsley	125 mL
1/2 lb	mozzarella cheese, shredded	250 g
1/4 cup	freshly grated Parmesan cheese	50 mL

In large pot of boiling salted water, cook penne for 8 to 10 minutes or until tender but firm. Drain and rinse under cold water; drain again and set aside.

In bowl, beat egg; mix in beef, bread crumbs and thyme. Shape into 1-inch (2.5 cm) balls.

In large heavy Dutch oven, heat oil over medium heat; cook meatballs, in batches if necessary, for about 10 minutes or until no longer pink inside. Drain off fat.

Add onion and green onions; cook for 2 minutes. Stir in garlic, green pepper, mushrooms, celery, oregano and basil; cook for 2 minutes.

Add tomato sauce, parsley, penne and half of the mozzarella cheese; stir gently to mix. Sprinkle with Parmesan and remaining mozzarella cheese. (*Casserole can be prepared to this point, covered and cooled in refrigerator and stored for up to 2 days, or frozen in airtight container for up to 3 months; thaw before continuing.*)

Bake, covered, in 350°F (180°C) oven for 20 minutes; uncover and bake for 10 to 15 minutes longer or until bubbly. Makes about 10 servings.

Veal Stew with Dill and Peppers

This full-flavored veal stew is wonderful with noodles or dumplings.
A quick sauté of red or green peppers adds a colorful garnish.

2 tbsp	vegetable oil	25 mL
1-1/2 lb	stewing veal	750 g
1 tsp	salt	5 mL
1/2 tsp	pepper	2 mL
1	onion, chopped	1
1	sweet green pepper, chopped	1
1 tbsp	all-purpose flour	15 mL
1 tsp	paprika	5 mL
2	tomatoes, peeled, seeded and chopped	2
1/2 cup	white wine	125 mL
2 tbsp	chopped fresh dill (or 2 tsp/10 mL dried dillweed)	25 mL
1/2 cup	chicken stock	125 mL
	GARNISH	
1 tbsp	vegetable oil	15 mL
1	small sweet red or green pepper, chopped	1
1/2 cup	sour cream	125 mL
2 tbsp	chopped fresh dill (optional)	25 mL

In large skillet, heat oil over high heat; cook veal, in batches, until browned all over. Remove to 6-cup (1.5 L) baking dish; sprinkle with salt and pepper.

Reduce heat to medium; cook onion and green pepper, stirring occasionally, for about 3 minutes or until onion is softened. Stir in flour and paprika; cook for 1 minute. Stir in tomatoes; cook, stirring, until softened.

Stir in wine and dill; bring to boil. Pour in stock; cook for 2 minutes. Pour over veal. Cover and bake in 325°F (160°C) oven for 1-1/2 hours or until veal is tender. *(Stew can be cooled in refrigerator and frozen in airtight container.)*

GARNISH: In skillet, heat oil over medium heat; cook red pepper until softened. Sprinkle over each serving of stew. Top with sour cream, and dill (if using). Makes 4 to 6 servings.

Oven-Roasted Parsnips

*Parsnips, one of the dependable winter standbys, add a golden color and a
delicate sweetness to any meal. Hutterites, early settlers on the Prairies, use melted goose fat
instead of butter to brush over the parsnips before baking.*

2 lb	parsnips	1 kg
1/4 cup	butter, melted	50 mL
	Salt and pepper	

Peel and trim parsnips; arrange in single layer in greased baking dish. Brush with butter; season with salt and pepper to taste.

❧ Cover and bake in 350°F (180°C) oven for 45 minutes. Uncover and bake for 30 minutes longer or until tender and golden. Makes 6 servings.

FREEZER-FRIENDLY FACTS

What a treat to open the freezer and know that there's a casserole waiting for spur-of-the moment entertaining. Weekends are often the only time these days to plan ahead and stock the freezer. Here are tips for the very best results with such freezer-to-oven recipes as Lamb Moussaka, Meatball and Penne Casserole and Veal Stew with Dill and Peppers (recipes, this chapter).

FREEZING TIPS
❧ *Use only high-quality fresh food.*
❧ *Handle, package and store food carefully.*
❧ *Cool all cooked foods quickly; freeze as soon as possible.*
❧ *Use masking tape to label and date all foods.*
❧ *Keep an inventory; when frozen, many foods look alike.*
❧ *Set freezer at 0°F (-18°C) or lower.*

PACKAGING POINTERS
❧ *Poorly packaged foods deteriorate in the freezer. They can develop freezer burn, a condition that results when air seeps into the package. This cannot be reversed by thawing.*
❧ *Polyethylene bags: These heavy-duty freezer bags are airtight, moisture-proof and vapor-proof. Freeze foods directly in them or use them to wrap casseroles for extra protection.*
❧ *Foil: Heavy-duty foil makes an airtight wrapping. Be careful not to puncture. Seal foil tightly around the edges.*
❧ *Freezing in serving dishes: Line casserole dishes with foil, then fill with cooked food. After freezing, remove the foil and contents; seal well and leave the dish free for other uses. Later, frozen contents can be reheated in the same dish.*

STORAGE STRATEGY
❧ *Good inventory control ensures freezer foods with maximum flavor and food value. Label and date frozen foods. Prepared casseroles can be frozen for up to three months. Use the earliest-dated foods first.*

REHEATING INSTRUCTIONS
❧ *Check the recipe; some dishes require thawing for 24 hours in the refrigerator before reheating for optimum taste. Some foods, however, are best transferred directly from freezer to oven.*
❧ *When reheating, watch for bubbling juices as a sign that the food is thoroughly heated through; check that the center is hot.*
❧ *For microwave reheating, a general rule of thumb is to cover the dish (do not use foil) and use medium power for 15 to 30 minutes, stirring occasionally. Check the manufacturer's instructions for your oven.*

(clockwise from top) Rice and "Peas," Jerk Roast Pork, Baked Plantains; (in center) roasted sweet potatoes

JAMAICAN PARTY PLAN

MENU

Cocktail Patties*	Rice and "Peas"*
Jerk Roast Pork*	Nutty Coleslaw*
Baked Plantains*	Jamaican Ginger Cake (recipe, page 28)
Roasted Sweet Potatoes	

*Recipes included

SCHEDULE

❧ Up to 4 days ahead, make and refrigerate Jerk Marinade.

❧ The day before the party, make patties; refrigerate.

❧ Twelve hours ahead, marinate pork and make cake.

❧ Up to 4 hours ahead, make and refrigerate coleslaw.

❧ Two hours before serving, start roasting pork.

❧ As guests arrive, bake patties.

Jerk Roast Pork

Take your taste buds on a fantasy holiday and include your friends, too, with this typical Jamaican meal. Jerk food is peppery with allspice and so reminiscent of the Island in the Sun.

1	pork roast (about 3 lb/1.5 kg)	1
	JERK MARINADE	
4	green onions, chopped	4
3	cloves garlic	3
1	Scotch bonnet pepper or hot pepper, halved	1
1	onion, chopped	1
1/4 cup	orange juice	50 mL
3 tbsp	soy sauce	50 mL
1 tbsp	vegetable oil	15 mL
2 tsp	ground allspice	10 mL
2 tsp	white vinegar	10 mL
1/2 tsp	dried thyme	2 mL
1/2 tsp	each salt and pepper	2 mL
1/4 tsp	each curry powder and cinnamon	1 mL

JERK MARINADE: In food processor, purée together green onions, garlic, Scotch bonnet pepper, onion, orange juice, soy sauce, oil, allspice, vinegar, thyme, salt, pepper, curry powder and cinnamon. (*Marinade can be refrigerated in airtight container for up to 4 days.*)

In bowl, pour marinade over pork; cover and marinate in refrigerator for at least 2 hours or up to 12 hours, turning occasionally. Let stand at room temperature for 30 minutes.

Place pork on rack in roasting pan; roast in 325°F (160°C) oven for 1-3/4 to 2 hours or until meat thermometer registers 160°F (70°C). Transfer to warm platter and tent with foil; let stand for 10 minutes. Makes 8 servings.

TIPS: Pork shoulder or roasts are moist and tasty but not as attractive as easy-to-carve loin rib crown-style roasts that are partially boned.

Scotch bonnet peppers are fiery-hot peppers that add taste and heat to food. Wear disposable rubber gloves when handling. Do *not* touch any part of your body. Substitute jalapeño, banana peppers or hot green chilies.

Rice and "Peas"

What Canadians call red kidney beans, Jamaicans know as "peas."

1/2 cup	chopped bacon	125 mL
4	green onions, chopped	4
1	clove garlic, minced	1
1	sweet green pepper, chopped	1
3 cups	chicken stock	750 mL
1	can (400 mL) unsweetened coconut milk	1
1	can (19 oz/540 mL) red kidney beans, drained and rinsed	1
1	Scotch bonnet pepper or pinch cayenne pepper	1
1/2 tsp	dried thyme	2 mL
2 cups	parboiled rice	500 mL
	Salt	

In large heavy saucepan, cook bacon over medium heat for about 4 minutes or until crisp; drain off fat.

Add green onions, garlic and green pepper; cook, stirring occasionally, for 3 minutes. Add chicken stock, coconut milk, kidney beans, Scotch bonnet pepper and thyme; bring to boil.

Stir in rice; return to boil. Cover and reduce heat to low; cook for about 25 minutes or until rice is tender and liquid absorbed. Discard whole Scotch bonnet pepper. Fluff with fork; season with salt to taste. Makes 8 servings.

BAKED PLANTAINS

A large yellow banana-like vegetable with dark speckles, plantain needs cooking to be edible. To bake, peel 2 plantains; cut into thirds crosswise on diagonal. Brush lightly with oil; place in baking dish. Bake in 325°F (160°C) oven for 40 minutes or until soft. Slice thickly. Makes 8 servings.

Cocktail Patties

These spicy hand-held Jamaican meat pies are great make-aheads for casual get-togethers.

2 cups	all-purpose flour	500 mL
1-1/2 tsp	baking powder	7 mL
1 tsp	curry powder	5 mL
1/2 tsp	turmeric	2 mL
1/2 tsp	salt	2 mL
2/3 cup	shortening	150 mL
1/4 cup	butter	50 mL
1/3 cup	(approx) ice water	75 mL
	FILLING	
2 tsp	vegetable oil	10 mL
1	small onion, chopped	1
3	green onions, chopped	3
2	cloves garlic, minced	2
1 tbsp	minced Scotch bonnet pepper (or 1/4 tsp/1 mL cayenne pepper)	15 mL
1 lb	ground beef	500 g
1 tbsp	curry powder	15 mL
1 tsp	dried thyme	5 mL
1/2 tsp	turmeric	2 mL
1/4 tsp	each salt and pepper	1 mL
1 cup	water	250 mL
1/2 cup	fresh bread crumbs	125 mL

In large bowl, stir together flour, baking powder, curry powder, turmeric and salt; with pastry blender or two knives, cut in shortening and butter until crumbly. Drizzle in ice water, stirring with fork and adding up to 2 tbsp (25 mL) more water if necessary, to make soft dough. Form into ball; flatten into disc. Wrap and chill for 1 hour. (*Dough can be refrigerated for up to 5 days or frozen for up to 3 weeks.*)

🍴 FILLING: In skillet, heat oil over medium-high heat; cook onion, green onions, garlic and Scotch bonnet pepper for 3 minutes or until softened. Remove with slotted spoon and set aside.

🍴 Increase heat to high; cook beef, breaking up with back of spoon, for 5 minutes or until no longer pink. Drain off fat. Return onion mixture to pan along with curry powder, thyme, turmeric, salt and pepper; cook over medium heat, stirring occasionally, for 3 minutes.

🍴 Pour in water; bring to boil. Stir in bread crumbs; simmer for 3 minutes or until slightly thickened but still juicy. Let cool. (*Filling can be refrigerated in airtight container for up to 1 day.*)

🍴 Divide dough into 16 pieces. On lightly floured surface or floured pastry cloth and using stockinette-covered rolling pin, roll out each piece into 5-inch (12 cm) circle.

🍴 Brush edge on one half with water; place 2 heaping tbsp (25 mL) filling in center. Fold dough over filling, pressing edges together with fork to seal. Prick twice; place on ungreased baking sheet. (*Patties can be prepared to this point, covered and refrigerated for up to 1 day.*) Bake in 375°F (190°C) oven for 20 minutes or until crisp and golden. Makes 16 patties.

Nutty Coleslaw

Traditional coleslaw gets a kick with a dash of hot pepper sauce.

6 cups	finely shredded cabbage	1.5 L
1 cup	shredded carrots	250 mL
4	green onions, chopped	4
2/3 cup	light sour cream	150 mL
1/2 cup	light mayonnaise	125 mL
4 tsp	cider vinegar	20 mL
Dash	hot pepper sauce	Dash
1/2 cup	chopped walnuts, toasted	125 mL
1/4 tsp	salt	1 mL

In large serving bowl, toss together cabbage, carrots and green onions.

🍴 Stir together sour cream, mayonnaise, vinegar and hot pepper sauce; pour over cabbage mixture and toss to combine. Cover and refrigerate for up to 4 hours.

🍴 Just before serving, stir in walnuts and salt. Makes 8 servings.

Saucy Seasoned Sole

*For company fare or a special family dinner, try these fish fillets rolled around a
seasoned stuffing, then baked in a cheese and tomato sauce for extra flavor. Add a fresh
green vegetable and a favorite salad to round out the meal.*

2 cups	fresh bread cubes (1/4 inch/5 mm)	500 mL
2 tbsp	butter	25 mL
1 cup	chopped mushrooms	250 mL
1/2 cup	finely chopped celery	125 mL
1	clove garlic, minced	1
	Salt and pepper	
1-1/2 lb	sole or turbot fillets	750 g
2 tbsp	minced onion	25 mL
2 tbsp	chopped fresh parsley	25 mL
	CHEESE SAUCE	
1/4 cup	butter	50 mL
1/4 cup	all-purpose flour	50 mL
2 cups	milk	500 mL
1/2 cup	shredded old Cheddar cheese	125 mL
1/2 cup	chopped drained canned tomatoes	125 mL
1/4 tsp	dried oregano	1 mL
1/4 tsp	each salt and pepper	1 mL

CHEESE SAUCE: In saucepan, melt butter over medium heat; stir in flour and cook, stirring, for 3 minutes. Gradually whisk in milk until smooth; cook, whisking, for 5 to 7 minutes or until thickened. Reduce heat and simmer for 1 minute. Stir in Cheddar cheese, tomatoes, oregano, salt and pepper. Set aside.

❧ Spread bread cubes on baking sheet; bake in 350°F (180°C) oven for 10 to 12 minutes or until dry but not browned. Set aside.

❧ In skillet, melt butter over medium heat; cook mushrooms, celery and garlic for 5 minutes or until softened. Stir in 1/4 cup (50 mL) of the sauce; stir in bread cubes. Season with salt and pepper to taste.

❧ Divide bread mixture among fish fillets, spreading almost to edges; roll up jelly roll-style, fastening with toothpicks if necessary. Arrange rolls in single layer in shallow greased baking dish.

❧ Add onion and parsley to remaining sauce; pour over rolls. Bake in 350°F (180°C) oven for 30 minutes or until fish flakes easily when tested with fork. Makes 6 servings.

Lemon-Roasted Salmon

Lemon-Roasted Salmon

Elegant but refreshingly simple, a whole roasted salmon is sure to impress a crowd. Salmon is equally delicious served cold; just chill it before skinning, then serve with a dollop of creamy dill sauce.

1	salmon, cleaned (5 lb/2.2 kg)	1
1/4 tsp	each salt and pepper	1 mL
3	lemons, sliced	3
1/2 cup	each fresh dill and parsley sprigs	125 mL
2 tbsp	butter, melted	25 mL
	CREAMY DILL WINE SAUCE	
2 tbsp	butter	25 mL
2 tbsp	all-purpose flour	25 mL
1/2 cup	each milk, dry white wine and whipping cream	125 mL
3/4 tsp	salt	4 mL
1/4 tsp	pepper	1 mL
1/4 cup	chopped fresh dill	50 mL

Using sharp chef's knife, cut off fish head behind gills (or have fishmonger remove it). Rinse fish and pat dry. Season inside and out with salt and pepper. Arrange one-third of the lemon slices in lengthwise row along center of foil-lined baking sheet. Top with salmon.

❧ Fill body cavity with dill, parsley and another third of the lemons. Brush butter over salmon; top with remaining lemons. Crumple up foil around fish to hold juices, leaving salmon uncovered.

❧ Bake in 450°F (230°C) oven for about 45 minutes or until flesh at thickest part is opaque and flakes easily when tested with fork. Tent with foil; let stand for 5 minutes. Remove 1/4 cup (50 mL) pan juices; set aside.

❧ CREAMY DILL WINE SAUCE: In saucepan, melt butter over medium heat; stir in flour and cook, stirring, for 1 minute. Gradually whisk in milk, wine, cream, salt and pepper; cook, whisking, for 5 minutes. Stir in reserved pan juices; reduce heat and simmer for 5 minutes. Keep warm over low heat while carving salmon; stir in dill.

❧ To serve salmon, discard lemon on top. Cut lengthwise along backbone through to bone; gently pull off skin and discard. Cut along midline, parallel to backbone through to bone. Cut crosswise into 4-inch (10 cm) wide portions. Lift portions off bones to warm serving plates.

❧ Gently lift exposed bones away from other side. Cut salmon into portions; ease away from skin. Serve with warm sauce. Makes 12 servings.

Thai Chicken Fingers

Set the stage for entertaining with these delightful appetizers.

1 lb	boneless skinless chicken breasts	500 g
1 tbsp	sesame oil	15 mL
	PEANUT DIP	
3 tbsp	smooth peanut butter	50 mL
2 tbsp	Thai fish sauce or soy sauce	25 mL
2 tbsp	rice vinegar or lemon juice	25 mL
2 tbsp	liquid honey	25 mL
1 tbsp	hoisin sauce	15 mL
1 tbsp	sesame oil	15 mL

PEANUT DIP: In small bowl, blend together peanut butter, fish sauce, vinegar, honey, hoisin sauce and oil. Thin with up to 2 tbsp (25 mL) water if desired.

❧ Separate fillets from chicken breasts; cut remaining chicken into same-size pieces to make total of 20 strips. Pat dry. Brush with sesame oil.

❧ Grill chicken on greased grill over medium-high heat or broil for 3 to 4 minutes or until no longer pink inside. Serve with dip. Makes 20 appetizers.

White Bean Spread and Pita Crisps

This easy appetizer is sure to win raves from your guests. Serve with vegetables,
or rice or water crackers, in addition to the pita triangles.

1/3 cup	olive oil	75 mL
3	large cloves garlic, minced	3
3/4 tsp	ground coriander	4 mL
1/2 tsp	each salt and pepper	2 mL
3	pita breads	3
1	can (19 oz/540 mL) white kidney beans, drained and rinsed	1
1/4 cup	lemon juice	50 mL
1 tbsp	tahini	15 mL
1/2 tsp	ground cumin	2 mL
1/2 tsp	hot pepper sauce	2 mL
3 tbsp	chopped fresh coriander	50 mL

Stir together 2 tbsp (25 mL) of the olive oil, one-third of the garlic, 1/4 tsp (1 mL) of the ground coriander and pinch each of the salt and pepper.

🍃 Cut pitas into 6 rounds; cut into triangles and place on baking sheet. Brush triangles with olive oil mixture. Bake in 350°F (180°C) oven for 8 to 10 minutes or until crisp.

🍃 Meanwhile, in food processor, purée together remaining olive oil, garlic, ground coriander, salt and pepper, kidney beans, lemon juice, tahini, cumin and hot pepper sauce. Stir in fresh coriander. *(Spread can be refrigerated in airtight container for up to 2 days.)* Serve with pita crisps. Makes 2 cups (500 mL).

TIP: Tahini is a thick paste of ground sesame seeds available at Middle Eastern and specialty food stores.

Smoked Salmon Pâté

This smooth spread is perfect on pumpernickel bread, crackers or cucumber slices.

1/2 lb	smoked salmon	250 g
1	pkg (125 g) light cream cheese	1
2 tbsp	light mayonnaise	25 mL
1 tbsp	lemon juice	15 mL
1/4 cup	chopped green onions	50 mL
1 tbsp	chopped fresh dill	15 mL
1/4 tsp	pepper	1 mL

In food processor, purée together salmon, cream cheese, mayonnaise and lemon juice until smooth.

🍃 Mix in onions, dill and pepper. *(Pâté can be refrigerated in airtight container for up to 2 days.)* Makes about 2 cups (500 mL).

TIP: Smoked trout may be substituted for salmon.

FOR DIPS AND SPREADS

WONTON CRISPS
🍃 *Cut each of 24 wonton wrappers (1/2 lb/250 g) diagonally in half; arrange in single layer on ungreased baking sheets. Brush lightly with vegetable oil; sprinkle with 1/4 cup (50 mL) freshly grated Parmesan cheese and 1 tsp (5 mL) dried rosemary or basil.*

🍃 *Bake in 350°F (180°C) oven for 6 to 8 minutes or until puffy and crisp. Let cool; store in airtight container. Makes 48 crisps.*
HOMEMADE MELBA TOAST
🍃 *Remove crusts from thin slices of white or brown bread. Cut into serving-size pieces.*
🍃 *Bake on baking sheet in 275°F (140°C) oven, turning slices often,*

forabout 20 minutes or until browned and crisp.
CRUDITÉS
🍃 *Use fresh crunchy vegetables for dipping. Mix and match broccoli or cauliflower florets, diagonally sliced carrots, sticks of jicama or celery, snow peas, whole mushrooms, radishes, cherry tomatoes and skinny green beans.*

White Bean Spread, Pita Crisps and crudités

Eggs Benedict with Salmon, Fresh Fruit Salad with Lime Cream

WEEKEND BRUNCH FOR EIGHT

MENU

Raspberry Champagne

Fresh Fruit Salad with Lime Cream*

Assorted Muffins

Eggs Benedict with Salmon*

Steamed Asparagus

Mixed Greens with Classic Vinaigrette (recipe, page 13)

Rhubarb Custard Torte*

*Recipes included

Eggs Benedict with Salmon

Smoked salmon and rye bread add a new twist to this classic.

8	slices rye or pumpernickel bread, toasted and buttered	8
8	thin slices smoked salmon	8
8	hot poached eggs	8
	Yogurt Hollandaise (recipe follows)	
	Fresh parsley sprigs	
	Capers	

YOGURT HOLLANDAISE		
3/4 cup	plain low-fat yogurt	175 mL
2 tsp	lemon juice	10 mL
3	egg yolks	3
1/2 tsp	Dijon mustard	2 mL
1/4 tsp	each salt and granulated sugar	1 mL
Pinch	pepper	Pinch
Dash	hot pepper sauce	Dash

Place hot slices of toast on warm plates. Top each with slice of smoked salmon, then hot poached egg. Drizzle with Yogurt Hollandaise. Garnish with parsley and capers. Makes 8 servings.

TIP: Warm the plates and toast the bread while you poach the eggs.

⚜ In top of double boiler, whisk together yogurt, lemon juice, egg yolks, mustard, salt, sugar, pepper and hot pepper sauce; cook over simmering water, stirring constantly, for 6 to 8 minutes or until sauce is thick enough to coat back of spoon. *(Sauce can be set aside at room temperature for up to 1 hour; reheat gently in double boiler.)* Makes 1 cup (250 mL).

Fresh Fruit Salad with Lime Cream

A dollop of lime-flavored cream and a bit of liqueur turn a simple fruit salad into company fare. Serve at room temperature for best flavor.

2 cups	seedless green grapes, halved	500 mL
2 cups	orange segments (about 4 oranges)	500 mL
2 cups	sliced peeled kiwifruit (about 7)	500 mL
2 cups	red grapefruit segments (about 2 grapefruits)	500 mL
1/4 cup	granulated sugar	50 mL
1/4 cup	orange juice	50 mL
1/4 cup	orange liqueur or orange juice	50 mL
	LIME CREAM	
2/3 cup	whipping cream	150 mL
2 tsp	icing sugar	10 mL
2 tsp	grated lime rind (optional)	10 mL
2 tbsp	sour cream	25 mL

In 8-cup (2 L) glass bowl, layer grapes, oranges, kiwifruit and grapefruit. Sprinkle with sugar; sprinkle with orange juice and liqueur. Do not stir. Cover and refrigerate for at least 1 hour or up to 12 hours.

⚜ LIME CREAM: Up to 1 hour before serving, whip cream with icing sugar, and lime rind (if using) for 1 minute. Add sour cream; beat for 3 minutes.

⚜ Spoon fruit into individual bowls; top with dollop of lime cream. Makes 8 servings.

Rhubarb Custard Torte

This elegant torte with its tender shortbread crust is a great way to enjoy the first fruit of spring.

3/4 cup	butter, softened	175 mL
1/3 cup	granulated sugar	75 mL
2	egg yolks	2
2 cups	all-purpose flour	500 mL
1 tsp	baking powder	5 mL
1/2 tsp	salt	2 mL
	FILLING	
6 cups	coarsely chopped rhubarb (about 1-1/2 lb/750 g)	1.5 L
1/2 cup	granulated sugar	125 mL
1/4 cup	quick-cooking tapioca	50 mL
1/2 tsp	cinnamon	2 mL
6	eggs	6
2 cups	sour cream	500 mL
1/2 cup	packed brown sugar	125 mL
2 tsp	finely grated lemon rind	10 mL
1 tsp	vanilla	5 mL
	Icing sugar	
	Grated lemon rind	

In large bowl, beat butter with sugar; beat in egg yolks until light and fluffy. Stir together flour, baking powder and salt; add to egg mixture, mixing with hands until crumbly. Press two-thirds of the mixture onto bottom of 10-inch (3 L) springform pan. Bake in 400°F (200°C) oven for 10 minutes or just until light golden. Let cool. Press remaining mixture up side of pan.

❧ FILLING: In heavy stainless steel saucepan, combine rhubarb, granulated sugar, tapioca and cinnamon; let stand for 15 minutes. Stir in 1/4 cup (50 mL) water; bring to boil. Reduce heat to medium-low; cover and cook, stirring often, for about 10 minutes or until thickened and rhubarb is tender but not mushy. Let cool slightly; pour over crust.

❧ In large bowl, whisk eggs for about 2 minutes or until frothy; stir in sour cream, brown sugar, lemon rind and vanilla. Pour over rhubarb; bake in 350°F (180°C) oven for about 1 hour or until top is golden and custard is set. Let cool; cover and refrigerate for at least 3 hours or up to 12 hours.

❧ To serve, run sharp knife around crust; remove ring of pan. Sprinkle icing sugar over top and lemon rind in center of torte. Makes 8 servings.

Jamaican Ginger Cake

Fancy up this gingery cake with fresh pineapple and mango slices doused with orange juice, rum and coarsely grated orange rind. Top with rum-kissed whipped cream.

1 cup	butter, softened	250 mL
1-1/4 cups	packed brown sugar	300 mL
4	eggs	4
1/4 cup	grated gingerroot	50 mL
1 tsp	vanilla	5 mL
2-1/2 cups	all-purpose flour	625 mL
4 tsp	ground ginger	20 mL
4 tsp	baking powder	20 mL
1-1/2 tsp	cinnamon	7 mL
1/2 tsp	salt	2 mL
1 cup	milk	250 mL
	Icing sugar	

In large bowl, beat butter with sugar until fluffy; beat in eggs, one at a time, beating well after each addition. Stir in gingerroot and vanilla.

❧ Stir together flour, ground ginger, baking powder, cinnamon and salt; add to egg mixture alternately with milk, making three additions of dry ingredients and two of milk.

❧ Pour into greased 9-inch (3 L) Bundt or angel food cake pan, pressing batter slightly higher at edges. Bake in 350°F (180°C) oven for about 45 minutes or until cake tester inserted in center comes out clean. Let cool in pan on rack. Turn out onto serving plate; dust with icing sugar. Makes 8 servings.

Bumbleberry Pie

Nothing will create more of a spectacle than this pie — a tumble of apples, blueberries, raspberries, cranberries and plums baked under a scattering of pastry cutouts. Serve with a dollop of Chantilly cream — lightly whipped cream sweetened with brown sugar.

	Pastry for 10-inch (25 cm) double-crust pie (see Perfect Pastry, page 138)	
2-1/2 cups	diced peeled apples	625 mL
2 cups	blueberries	500 mL
2 cups	raspberries	500 mL
1-1/2 cups	blackberries	375 mL
1-1/2 cups	cranberries	375 mL
1-1/2 cups	diced plums	375 mL
1-1/4 cups	granulated sugar	300 mL
1/3 cup	all-purpose flour	75 mL
3 tbsp	cornstarch	50 mL
1/2 tsp	cinnamon	2 mL
1 tbsp	lemon juice	15 mL
1	egg, lightly beaten	1

On lightly floured surface, roll out a little more than half of the pastry; fit into 10-inch (25 cm) pie plate. Trim and flute edge. Roll out remaining dough. Using maple leaf cutter, cut out shapes; chill on baking sheet.

🍃 In large saucepan, combine apples, blueberries, raspberries, blackberries, cranberries and plums. Stir together sugar, flour, cornstarch and cinnamon; gently stir into fruit mixture along with lemon juice. Cook over medium heat, stirring occasionally, for about 5 minutes or until berries release juices. Spoon into prepared pie shell.

🍃 Arrange pastry leaves over filling. Brush crust and leaves with egg. Bake on baking sheet in 400°F (200°C) oven for 15 minutes. Reduce heat to 350°F (180°C); bake for about 50 minutes longer or until pastry is golden and filling is bubbling and thickened. Let cool on rack. Makes 8 servings.

TIP: Use fresh or frozen berries; increase baking time by 15 minutes if using frozen. If blackberries are unavailable, substitute raspberries or blueberries.

Frozen Citrus Cream with Orange Sauce

Frozen in a small mixing bowl, this citrusy make-ahead dessert is simple to prepare.
Serve in wedges with an orange sauce for a sublime ending to an entertaining dinner.

1 cup	granulated sugar	250 mL
1/4 cup	butter	50 mL
1 tbsp	grated orange rind	15 mL
3/4 cup	orange juice	175 mL
1 tsp	grated lemon rind	5 mL
1/4 cup	lemon juice	50 mL
3	eggs	3
1-1/2 cups	whipping cream	375 mL
	Orange Sauce (recipe follows)	

In heavy saucepan, whisk together sugar, butter, orange rind and juice, lemon rind and juice and eggs; cook over medium heat, whisking constantly, for 10 to 15 minutes or just until boiling. Transfer to bowl; let cool to room temperature.

❧ In separate bowl, beat whipping cream; fold into cooled orange mixture. Spoon into small mixing bowl lined with plastic wrap. Freeze for at least 4 hours or until firm, or for up to 12 hours.

❧ To unmould, invert onto serving platter; remove bowl and plastic wrap. Slice into wedges. Serve with Orange Sauce. Makes 8 servings.

ORANGE SAUCE

2 cups	orange juice	500 mL
1/2 cup	granulated sugar	125 mL
1 tbsp	cornstarch	15 mL
1 tbsp	lemon juice	15 mL

❧ In saucepan, whisk together orange juice, sugar, cornstarch and lemon juice; cook over medium heat, stirring often, for about 10 minutes or until thickened. Refrigerate for at least 2 hours or for up to 2 days. Makes about 1-1/2 cups (375 mL).

Caramel Snaps

These crispy, candylike wafers are a perfect complement to the
Frozen Citrus Cream dessert (above).

1/4 cup	packed brown sugar	50 mL
1/4 cup	corn syrup	50 mL
3 tbsp	butter	50 mL
1/2 tsp	vanilla	2 mL
1/2 cup	all-purpose flour	125 mL
1/4 cup	sliced almonds	50 mL
3/4 tsp	ground cardamom	4 mL

In saucepan, cook sugar, corn syrup and butter over medium heat, stirring, until boiling. Stir in vanilla. Let cool slightly.

❧ Stir together flour, almonds and cardamom; stir into brown sugar mixture until well combined.

❧ Drop by teaspoonfuls (5 mL), at least 4 inches (10 cm) apart, on parchment paper-lined baking sheets. Bake in 350°F (180°C) oven for 6 to 8 minutes or until golden brown. Let cool for 5 minutes. Remove to rack; let cool completely. (*Snaps can be stored in airtight container for up to 2 days.*) Makes about 30 cookies.

Mocha Marjolaine

This traditional French dessert makes a fabulous frozen finish to a special meal for company.

1-1/2 cups	toasted hazelnuts	375 mL
1 cup	granulated sugar	250 mL
2 cups	toasted sliced almonds	500 mL
2 tbsp	cornstarch	25 mL
7	egg whites	7
1/2 tsp	cream of tartar	2 mL
8 oz	semisweet chocolate	250 g
3 cups	whipping cream	750 mL
1 tbsp	instant coffee granules	15 mL
1 tbsp	granulated sugar	15 mL
	Whole hazelnuts (optional)	

Line 17- x 11-inch (45 x 29 cm) rimmed baking sheet with parchment paper. Draw three 16- x 3-inch (40 x 8 cm) rectangles on paper; turn paper over.

⁂ In food processor, finely grind hazelnuts with 1/3 cup (75 mL) of the sugar; transfer to bowl. Set aside 1 cup (250 mL) of the almonds for garnish. In food processor, finely grind remaining almonds with 1/3 cup (75 mL) of the sugar; stir into hazelnuts along with cornstarch.

⁂ In large bowl, beat egg whites with cream of tartar until soft peaks form; gradually beat in remaining sugar until stiff peaks form. Fold in nut mixture in three additions. Evenly spread over rectangles; bake in 275°F (140°C) oven for 1-1/2 hours or until golden. Let meringues cool on rack.

⁂ Meanwhile, coarsely chop 6 oz (175 g) of the chocolate; place in bowl. In saucepan, bring 1/2 cup (125 mL) of the cream to boil; pour over chocolate, stirring until melted. Refrigerate ganache for 30 minutes or until spreadable.

⁂ Meanwhile, chop remaining chocolate; melt in double boiler over hot (not boiling) water. Let cool. Whip 2 cups (500 mL) of the remaining cream; fold 2 tbsp (25 mL) into cooled chocolate. Fold back into whipped cream.

⁂ Stir together coffee granules, sugar and 1 tbsp (15 mL) hot water until dissolved; let cool slightly. In separate bowl, beat remaining whipped cream with coffee mixture. Set aside.

⁂ Gently remove meringues from parchment paper; trim with sharp knife if necessary to make uniform size. Place one of the meringues on serving platter; spread with one-third of the chilled ganache. Spread 1/4-inch (5 mm) thick layer of chocolate whipped cream over ganache.

⁂ Spread second meringue with half of the remaining ganache; place on top of first meringue. Spread coffee whipped cream over top. Spread remaining ganache over third meringue; place on top of coffee whipped cream. Spread enough of the remaining chocolate whipped cream to cover sides and top, leaving ends bare.

⁂ Pipe remaining chocolate whipped cream into rosettes on top. Garnish top with whole hazelnuts (if using) and sides with reserved almonds. Freeze for at least 4 hours or until solid. *(Marjolaine can be frozen for up to 2 days.)* Serve frozen. Makes 10 servings.

Chapter Two

Let the CELEBRATIONS BEGIN!

Match special occasions with memorable food. Choose a lovingly baked wedding cake, elegant finger food for showers, or desserts — from ice cream clowns for birthday kids to decadent chocolate pie for you.

One-Bowl Birthday Cake

Whether you're turning 40 or 4, a birthday cake is always part of the fun.
This one is all dressed in chocolate and ready to party.

2 cups	all-purpose flour	500 mL
1-1/4 cups	granulated sugar	300 mL
4 tsp	baking powder	20 mL
1/2 tsp	salt	2 mL
1 cup	milk	250 mL
1/2 cup	shortening	125 mL
1 tsp	almond extract	5 mL
3	eggs	3
1 cup	sweetened flaked coconut	250 mL
	Easy Chocolate Icing (recipe follows)	
	Coconut (optional)	

Grease and flour two 9-inch (1.5 L) round cake pans. Set aside.
🍃 In large bowl, stir together flour, sugar, baking powder and salt. Add 3/4 cup (175 mL) of the milk, shortening and almond extract; beat for 1 minute. Add remaining milk and eggs; beat for 1 minute or until smooth. Stir in coconut.

🍃 Pour into prepared pans; bake in 350°F (180°C) oven for 30 to 40 minutes or until cake tester inserted in center comes out clean. Let cool in pans for 5 minutes; turn out onto racks and let cool completely. Spread Easy Chocolate Icing between cake layers and over top and sides. Garnish with coconut (if using). Makes 10 servings.

VARIATION
🍃 COFFEE HAZELNUT CAKE: Add 4 tsp (20 mL) instant coffee granules dissolved in 1 tbsp (15 mL) water to milk. Add 1/2 cup (125 mL) chopped toasted hazelnuts instead of coconut to batter. Use vanilla instead of almond extract.

EASY CHOCOLATE ICING		
2 cups	chocolate chips	500 mL
1/2 cup	milk	125 mL
1/3 cup	butter, in bits	75 mL

🍃 In small saucepan, heat chocolate chips with milk over low heat, stirring, until melted and smooth. Remove from heat; stir in butter, a little at a time, until smooth. Pour into bowl and refrigerate until firm enough to spread, about 2 hours. Makes about 2 cups (500 mL).

CRISPY MARSHMALLOW CREATIONS

Cereal treats have long been favorites with both adults and kids — they're fast and easy to make and taste terrific. Here are some fun ideas for creating unique shapes for birthdays and other special occasions. Kids will delight in helping to make — and eat — the delicious results!

🔔 *In saucepan, melt 1/3 cup (75 mL) butter over low heat; stir in 7-1/2 cups (1.875 L) miniature marshmallows until melted. Remove from heat. Stir in 1 tsp (5 mL) vanilla and a few drops of desired food coloring; stir in 9 cups (2.25 L) crispy rice cereal. With wet hands, shape mixture into desired shape on baking sheet; decorate with candies, using icing as glue.*

🔔 *BIRTHDAYS: Mould the child's first initial or age. Or make a carousel cake as in photo: Line sides and bottoms of three 8-inch (1.2 L) round cake pans with waxed paper. Make two-thirds of the recipe desired color; press into 2 of the pans. Repeat with remaining ingredients, leaving uncolored; press into remaining pan. Let set. Remove from pans and peel off paper. Stack with uncolored layer in center; decorate.*

🔔 *CHRISTMAS: Form green triangle-shaped Christmas tree, with small square at bottom for trunk. Add colored sprinkles or candies for Christmas lights.*

🔔 *VALENTINE'S DAY: Form pink heart shape, using red food coloring. Decorate with cinnamon heart candies (unless serving to young children who might choke on them).*

🔔 *ST. PATRICK'S DAY: Try a green shamrock.*

🔔 *EASTER: Use yellow food coloring and form a chick.*

🔔 *HALLOWEEN: Delight little goblins with a crunchy orange jack-o'-lantern.*

TIP: If you plan to decorate your creations with candies, you will need a simple frosting to use as glue. Mix together 1-1/2 cups (375 mL) sifted icing sugar and 2 tbsp (25 mL) water, adding up to 2 tsp (10 mL) more water if necessary to make spreadable. Use a pastry brush or small spatula to dab this icing onto candies and set them in place. Let dry before serving.

HOME-BASED KIDS' PARTIES

Simple parties at home, where the birthday boy or girl can take the spotlight, are important events and won't blow the budget. With a little planning (how about fireworks in the snow, baking gingerbread cookies in July, Halloween costumes in the spring) and maybe some help from a teenage babysitter, your child can shine doing fun activities with favorite friends.

DECORATIONS
- Go wild with balloons and streamers.
- Use a colorful child's bedsheet or beach towel as a washable tablecloth.
- Hang stuffed animals, toy cars, dolls as decorations.
- Set out baseball cards for placecards.
- Make a welcoming banner with a streamer of computer paper. Add a personal message using bold, bright-colored markers and attach photographs of the birthday star at various stages and ages.

GAMES AND THEMES
- TEDDY BEARS' PICNIC: Invite children to bring their favorite stuffed toy. Provide plastic pails to carry individual picnic lunches. Go to the park or spread a blanket on the floor. Have a jelly-bean hunt. Once the lunch is finished, hand out matching shovels and adjourn to the sandbox or snow pile to play.
- DRESS-UP PARTY: Invite guests to wear costumes or provide a dress-up box for innovative creations. A Polaroid of each guest is nice to add to the goodie bags. Play Pass the Parcel: each time the music stops, the child in the circle holding the parcel gets to remove one layer of wrapping and claim

the candy or small favor underneath.
- PIRATE THEME: Offer a kerchief for each buccaneer to tie around his or her head, and a black eye patch to wear. A treasure hunt can be as simple or complicated as the party-goers' ages dictate. And the kerchiefs make good loot carriers.

PARTY FOOD
- For small-fry, small servings of simple familiar finger food are best. Peanut butter and banana sandwiches, cheese and fruit kabobs, veggies and dips (recipe, page 72) are winners.
- Older children like favorite standbys: pizza, burgers, hotdogs or filled bagels. Kids will have fun making pizza faces (recipe, opposite page).
- Dessert that appeals to any age is ice cream and birthday cake.

PARTY GOODIE BAGS

Little bags of take-home favors usually signal the end of the party. These needn't be expensive. Your child can help make them.

FOR THE BAGS:
- Apply stickers to small paper sandwich bags and write each guest's name on one.
- Recycle clean milk bags, tied with colored wool.
- Plastic shaped boxes or pencil cases can be picked up cheaply at discount stores.
- If you enjoy sewing, try making your own bags from fabric. Tied with string, these serve later for storing stones, marbles and dress-up jewelry.

FOR THE FAVORS:
- Funny-shaped or scented erasers, stickers, tiny storybooks, felt-tip washable markers, plastic dinosaurs or shaped notepads are winners.
- Candy seems to be essential: candy necklaces, gummy bears and worms or popcorn. After Halloween, small chocolate bars are often sold at a reduced price (freeze them), and quality candy shops greatly reduce the price of delicacies such as chocolate hockey pucks or white chocolate polar bears after Christmas.

FUNNY FACE PIZZAS

Carrots and zucchini for hair, a slice of sweet pepper for a smiling mouth, and pepperoni and olive slices for eyes — kids love adding their own special "features" before the pizza is popped into the oven. (See page 68 for Quick-Mixing Pizza Dough.)

Peanut Butter Faces

These are party sandwiches of an entirely different kind!
Let the guests make their own and see the creativity that results.

8	slices whole wheat bread	8
1/2 cup	peanut butter	125 mL
1-1/2 cups	shredded carrots	375 mL
Half	banana, sliced	Half
1/4 cup	raisins	50 mL
Half	sweet red pepper, cut into strips	Half
Quarter	English cucumber, sliced	Quarter

Spread each bread slice with peanut butter; place each slice on plate. Let guests decorate slices as desired with carrots for hair, banana for ears or eyes, raisins for nose or eyes, red pepper for mouth and cucumber for eyes. Makes 8 servings.

Ice Cream Clowns

A birthday party isn't complete without a clown. Ice cream clowns are a cool choice. They're easy to make and fun to eat.

4 oz	semisweet chocolate	125 g
6	pointed ice cream cones	6
1 cup	colored candy sprinkles	250 mL
6	large (4-inch/10 cm diameter) gingersnap cookies	6
6	large scoops ice cream	6
	Assorted candies (candy-coated chocolate, licorice allsorts and strings, chocolate sprinkles, jelly beans, gumdrops)	

In top of double boiler over hot (not boiling) water, melt chocolate; let cool slightly. Dip cones into chocolate, letting excess drip off. Sprinkle with colored candy sprinkles. Let stand, with points up, on waxed paper to dry.

❧ Place each cookie on plate; top with ice cream scoop. Place cone on ice cream to resemble clown's hat. Decorate ice cream "face" with candies to resemble eyes, nose, ears, mouth and hair. Freeze for at least 30 minutes or until solid. Makes 6 servings.

Almond Lemon Wedding Cake

Picture the bride and groom cutting into a tiered wedding cake that's lusciously iced and decorated with violets and scented geranium leaves. This cake is beautiful to behold yet simple to make.

1 cup	butter, softened	250 mL
2 cups	granulated sugar	500 mL
1 tbsp	grated lemon rind	15 mL
4 tsp	almond extract	20 mL
4	eggs	4
3 cups	all-purpose flour	750 mL
1-1/2 tsp	baking powder	7 mL
1 tsp	baking soda	5 mL
1 tsp	salt	5 mL
1 cup	ground almonds	250 mL
2 cups	sour cream	500 mL

	LEMON CREAM CHEESE ICING	
3 lb	cream cheese, softened	1.5 kg
1 cup	butter, softened	250 mL
2 tbsp	lemon juice	25 mL

8 cups	icing sugar, sifted	2 L
2 tbsp	grated lemon rind	25 mL
	GARNISH	
	Fresh or candied flowers	
	Lemon rind twists	

Grease and flour 8-cup (2 L) and 12-cup (3 L) cake pans. Line bottoms with waxed or parchment paper and set aside.

In very large bowl, beat together butter, sugar, lemon rind and almond extract until light and fluffy. Beat in eggs, one at a time, beating well after each addition.

In separate bowl, sift together flour, baking powder, baking soda and salt; stir in ground almonds. Stir into creamed mixture alternately with sour cream, making 3 additions of dry mixture and 2 additions of sour cream.

Pour 3 cups (750 mL) of the batter into small pan; pour

remaining batter into large pan. Tap pans lightly on counter to release excess air bubbles. Bake in 325°F (160°C) oven for 40 to 50 minutes or until cake tester inserted in center comes out clean. Let stand in pans for 10 minutes. Loosen edges and turn out onto racks. Remove waxed paper and let cool completely. Repeat recipe to make a total of 4 layers.

To level cakes, use ruler as guide and insert toothpicks around sides to mark even cutting line. With long serrated knife, cut off rounded tops. Remove tooth-picks. *(Cake layers can be wrapped and frozen for up to 1 month.)*

LEMON CREAM CHEESE ICING: In very large mixing bowl, beat together cream cheese, butter and lemon juice until fluffy. Gradually beat in icing sugar. Spoon 1-1/2 cups (375 mL) into piping bag fitted with star tip; set aside for decorating. Beat lemon rind into remaining icing.

Place one large layer, cut side up, on serving base; slip strips of waxed paper under cake to protect base from icing. Spread about 1-1/2 cups (375 mL) icing over top for filling. Top with second large layer, cut side down; spread icing over sides and top. Dip palette knife into hot water and smooth icing. Refrigerate until firm.

Place bottom layer of small tier on slightly smaller round of stiff foil-covered cardboard. Using about 3/4 cup (175 mL)

icing for filling, assemble and ice as per large tier.

Using same 8-cup (2 L) cake pan, trace outline on bot-tom tier. Cut 7 plastic straws exact height of bottom tier. Insert 5 evenly spaced straws 1 inch (2.5 cm) inside outline; insert remaining straw in center. Center top tier on bottom tier, using traced outline as guide.

Remove waxed paper strips. With reserved icing, pipe

CHAMPAGNE MIMOSAS

Half-fill a champagne flute or large wine goblet with fresh orange juice; top with champagne. Garnish with an orange slice or sprig of mint.

shell pattern around top and bottom edges of each tier. *(Cake can be prepared to this point and refrigerated for up to 2 days.)*

GARNISH: Just before serving, decorate cake with flow-ers and lemon rind twists. To serve, remove top tier with 2 metal spatulas and set aside. Following outside shape of cake, cut border about 2 inches (5 cm) from outside edge; cut border into small slices. Repeat once more. Cut center portion into wedges. Repeat with top tier, cutting only 1 bor-der. Makes 60 servings.

Queen Victoria popularized the white bridal gown at her wedding in 1840. Prior to that, brides rarely wore white.

Racks of Lamb with Lemon and Mint

Rack of lamb says special occasion. Two racks — Frenched to reveal the ribs, crisscrossed in a guard of honor arch, then roasted to pink perfection — say a very festive dinner for four.

2	**racks of lamb (each 3/4 lb/375 g)**	2
	LEMON MINT MARINADE	
2 tbsp	**chopped fresh mint (or 1 tsp/5 mL dried)**	25 mL
1 tsp	**grated lemon rind**	5 mL
2 tbsp	**lemon juice**	25 mL
1 tbsp	**vegetable oil**	15 mL
Pinch	**pepper**	Pinch

Place each rack of lamb, meaty side up, on cutting board. Using sharp paring knife, cut line across rack where meaty portion begins, about 3 inches (8 cm) down from rib ends. Cut off layer of fat between line and rib ends.

❧ Cut off meat and fat between bared ribs to expose bones. Scrape exposed rib bones clean, removing any remaining meat and fat. Trim fat from meaty portion of ribs to 1/8-inch (3 mm) thickness, lifting away fat as you work.

❧ With rib ends up, press racks together to interlink bones. Separate bases about 1 inch (2.5 cm) to stabilize; place in shallow dish.

❧ LEMON MINT MARINADE: Whisk together mint, lemon rind and juice, oil and pepper; brush over lamb. Let stand at room temperature for 30 minutes.

❧ Place lamb on greased rack in roasting pan; drizzle with any remaining marinade. Cover exposed ribs with foil to prevent charring. Roast in 450°F (230°C) oven for 10 minutes. Reduce heat to 325°F (160°C); roast for 40 minutes or until meat thermometer registers 140°F (60°C) for rare or 150°F (65°C) for medium-rare.

❧ Transfer to warm platter; tent with foil and let stand for 10 minutes. To serve, remove all foil; carve between bones. Makes 4 servings.

Spinach Parmesan Phyllo Triangles

Crisp phyllo pastry wraps a cheesy spinach filling — perfect for party nibbles.(Photo, page 44)

10	sheets phyllo pastry	10
1/3 cup	butter, melted	75 mL
	SPINACH PARMESAN FILLING	
1	pkg (10 oz/284 g) fresh spinach	1
2 tsp	vegetable oil	10 mL
1	small onion, finely chopped	1
2	cloves garlic, minced	2
1/4 cup	finely chopped sweet red pepper	50 mL
2/3 cup	freshly grated Parmesan cheese	150 mL
1/4 cup	cream cheese, softened	50 mL
1/2 tsp	grated lemon rind	2 mL
1/2 tsp	pepper	2 mL
1/4 tsp	salt	1 mL

SPINACH PARMESAN FILLING: Trim spinach and rinse under water; shake off excess water. In saucepan, cover spinach and cook over medium-high heat, with just the water clinging to leaves, for about 5 minutes or just until wilted. Drain well and squeeze dry; chop and place in bowl.

❧ In skillet, heat oil over medium heat; cook onion, garlic and red pepper for about 3 minutes or until softened. Add to spinach; stir in 1/3 cup (75 mL) of the Parmesan, cream cheese, lemon rind, pepper and salt. Set aside.

❧ Place 1 sheet of phyllo on work surface. Cover remaining phyllo with dampened tea towel to prevent drying out. Lightly brush phyllo sheet with butter. Place another sheet on top; brush lightly with butter. Sprinkle with heaping tablespoonful (15 mL) of the remaining Parmesan. Using sharp knife, cut sheets lengthwise into six 2-inch (5 cm) wide strips.

❧ Spoon 2 tsp (10 mL) of the filling about 1/2 inch (1 cm) from one end of each strip. Fold one corner of phyllo over filling so bottom edge meets side edge to form triangle. Fold up triangle. Continue folding triangle sideways and upward until end of phyllo strip. Working quickly, repeat with remaining ingredients.

❧ Transfer to baking sheet; brush lightly with butter. *(Triangles can be prepared to this point and frozen on baking sheets; store in airtight containers for up to 2 weeks. Do not thaw before baking.)* Bake in 375°F (190°C) oven for 20 minutes or until golden. Makes about 24 appetizers.

Curried Chicken Crunchies

Cooked with fragrant spices, then coated with a yogurt-mayonnaise mixture, this finger food suits any crowd or occasion. (Photo, page 43)

2	boneless skinless chicken breasts	2
3/4 tsp	curry powder	4 mL
1/2 tsp	turmeric	2 mL
1/4 tsp	ground cumin	1 mL
1/4 tsp	ground coriander	1 mL
Pinch	each salt and pepper	Pinch
2 tsp	vegetable oil	10 mL
2 tbsp	plain yogurt	25 mL
2 tbsp	light mayonnaise	25 mL
24	round blue corn chips or potato chips	24
4	radishes, thinly sliced	4
	Green onion tips	

Cut chicken into 1/2-inch (1 cm) cubes. Combine curry powder, turmeric, cumin, coriander, salt and pepper.

❧ In nonstick skillet, heat oil over medium heat; stir-fry spice mixture for 1 minute. Add chicken; cook, stirring, for about 5 minutes or until no longer pink inside. Remove from skillet; let cool. *(Chicken can be covered and refrigerated for up to 24 hours.)*

❧ In bowl, stir together chicken, yogurt and mayonnaise. Place 1 or 2 chicken pieces on each corn chip; garnish with radishes and green onions. Makes 24 appetizers.

Carrot Salad Bites

Make these delectable morsels the day before the big party.

1-1/2 cups	grated carrots	375 mL
1 tbsp	lemon juice	15 mL
1 tbsp	olive oil	15 mL
Pinch	each salt and pepper	Pinch
1/3 cup	herbed cream cheese	75 mL
12	slices rye cocktail bread	12
	Fresh parsley sprigs	
	Violets (optional)	

In bowl, stir together carrots, lemon juice, oil, salt and pepper. *(Mixture can be covered and refrigerated for up to 24 hours.)*

♣ Spread cream cheese over bread slices; place on serving tray. Divide carrot mixture among slices. Garnish with parsley, and violets (if using). Makes 12 appetizers.

Grilled Salmon Skewers

Hot or cold, these skewers of fresh salmon look and taste great.

1 lb	salmon fillet, skinned	500 g
1/4 cup	soy sauce	50 mL
1/4 cup	liquid honey	50 mL
1 tbsp	rice vinegar	15 mL
1 tsp	minced gingerroot	5 mL
1	clove garlic, minced	1
Pinch	pepper	Pinch
1	lemon, cut into 12 wedges (optional)	1

Slice salmon lengthwise into 12 long strips; thread each onto soaked wooden skewer. Place in shallow dish.

♣ Whisk together soy sauce, honey, vinegar, ginger, garlic and pepper; pour over skewers, turning to coat well. Let stand at room temperature for 30 minutes.

♣ Reserving marinade, thread 1 lemon wedge (if using) onto end of each skewer. Place on greased grill over medium-high heat. Cook, brushing often with marinade, for 4 minutes; turn and cook for 3 to 4 minutes or until fish flakes easily when tested with fork. Makes 12 appetizers.

Ginger Crab Cakes

This is a perfect little nibble to serve with other finger foods at a cocktail or tapas party.

2	pkg (each 7 oz/200 g) frozen crabmeat, thawed, drained and flaked	2
1/2 cup	light mayonnaise	125 mL
1/4 cup	minced green onions	50 mL
1 tbsp	chopped fresh coriander	15 mL
1 tbsp	lime juice	15 mL
2 tsp	minced gingerroot	10 mL
1/4 tsp	hot pepper sauce	1 mL
1/4 tsp	each salt and pepper	1 mL
2	eggs	2
3/4 cup	bread crumbs	175 mL
1/4 cup	vegetable oil	50 mL

In bowl, mix together crabmeat, mayonnaise, onions, coriander, lime juice, ginger, hot pepper sauce, salt and pepper. Shape into 12 patties.

♣ In shallow dish, lightly beat eggs. Place bread crumbs in another shallow dish. Dip patties into egg, then press into bread crumbs to coat all over.

♣ In skillet, heat 2 tbsp (25 mL) of the oil over medium heat; cook crab cakes, in batches and adding remaining oil as needed, for 2 minutes per side or until golden. Makes 12 appetizers.

Shrimp Canapés

Pretty to look at, delicious to eat, these canapés are simple to prepare.

12	large raw shrimp, peeled and deveined	12
12	slices pumpernickel cocktail bread	12
12	slices English cucumber (unpeeled)	12
3 tbsp	light mayonnaise	50 mL
1 tbsp	chopped fresh chives	15 mL
1/2 tsp	lemon juice	2 mL
Pinch	each salt and pepper	Pinch
	Chopped fresh chives	
	Sliced lemon bits (optional)	

In large saucepan of simmering salted water, poach shrimp for 2 to 3 minutes or just until pink. Drain well and let cool. *(Shrimp can be covered and refrigerated for up to 8 hours.)*

🦐 Place bread slices on serving tray; top each with cucumber slice, then shrimp.

🦐 Stir together mayonnaise, chives, lemon juice, salt and pepper; dot on top of each shrimp. Garnish with chives, and lemon (if using). Makes 12 appetizers.

TIP: If fresh chives are not available, use chopped fresh dill or parsley.

(clockwise from top) Grilled Salmon Skewers, Shrimp Canapés, Ginger Crab Cakes, Carrot Salad Bites and Curried Chicken Crunchies (p. 41)

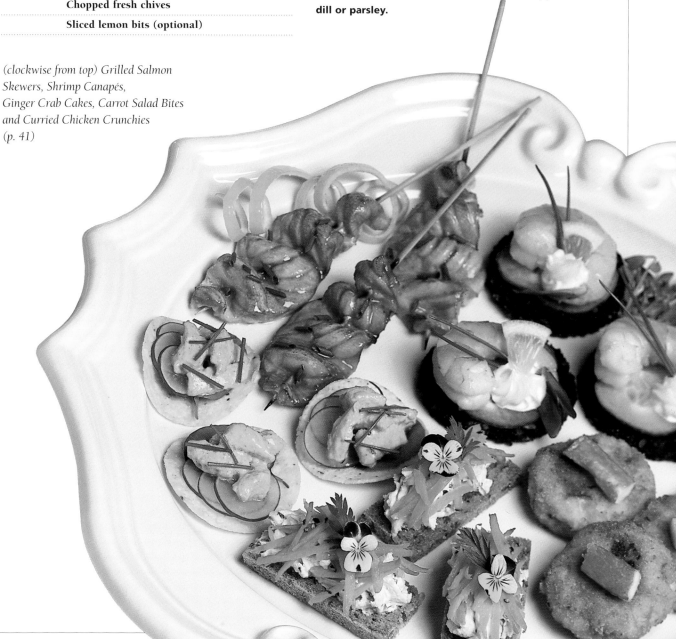

(from left) Lobster Pockets, Spinach Parmesan Phyllo Triangles (p. 41), Brie and Pecan Tarts and Mini Crab Quiches

Lobster Pockets

These dilly mini pockets can be partially prepared the day before. Use enough leaf lettuce to add a pretty frill.

1	can (11.3 oz/320 g) frozen lobster meat, thawed	1
1/2 cup	chopped celery	125 mL
1/2 cup	diced carrot	125 mL
1/2 cup	chopped radishes	125 mL
1/4 cup	finely chopped green onions	50 mL
1/2 cup	light mayonnaise	125 mL
1/3 cup	light sour cream	75 mL
2 tbsp	chopped fresh dill	25 mL
1 tbsp	lemon juice	15 mL
Dash	hot pepper sauce	Dash
	Salt and pepper	
36	mini pitas	36
	Torn leaf lettuce	

Drain lobster meat; squeeze dry and shred into bowl. Add celery, carrot, radishes and green onions. (*Filling can be prepared to this point, covered and refrigerated for up to 1 day; drain before continuing.*)

ஓ Stir together mayonnaise, sour cream, dill, lemon juice and hot pepper sauce; stir into lobster mixture. Season with salt and pepper to taste.

ஓ Slit opening in pitas; line with lettuce. Spoon lobster mixture into pitas. (*Pockets can be covered with plastic wrap and refrigerated for up to 2 hours.*) Makes 36 appetizers.

Mini Crab Quiches

Tiny bite-size quiches are always in vogue and are easily made ahead and frozen.

	Pastry (recipe follows)	
1/2 cup	milk	125 mL
1/2 cup	herbed cream cheese	125 mL
2	eggs, beaten	2
1/4 tsp	each salt and hot pepper sauce	1 mL
Pinch	pepper	Pinch
1	pkg (7 oz/200 g) frozen crabmeat, thawed, drained and flaked	1
	Sliced green onions	

On lightly floured surface, roll out pastry to 1/8-inch (3 mm) thickness; cut out thirty-six 5-inch (12 cm) rounds. Fit into 2-1/4-inch (6 cm) tart tins. Prick shells in several places with fork. Refrigerate for 30 minutes. Bake in 375°F (190°C) oven for 15 minutes.

TIP: Change the flavor by using 1 cup (250 mL) chopped smoked ham instead of crab.

In saucepan, heat milk over medium-high heat until bubbles form around edge; stir in cream cheese until melted. Remove from heat.

In bowl, whisk 2 tbsp (25 mL) of the milk mixture into eggs; gradually stir in remaining milk mixture. Stir in salt, hot pepper sauce and pepper; mix in crab.

Spoon filling into pastry shells; bake for 12 minutes or until puffed and just set. Run knife around edges; remove from tins.

(Quiches can be prepared to this point, cooled, layered between waxed paper in airtight container and frozen for up to 2 weeks. Reheat, frozen, on baking sheet in 375°F/190°C oven for 15 minutes or until heated through.) Garnish with onions. Makes 36 appetizers.

	PASTRY	
3 cups	all-purpose flour	750 mL
1 tsp	salt	5 mL
1/2 cup	cold butter, cubed	125 mL
1/2 cup	cold lard or shortening, cubed	125 mL
1	egg	1
2 tsp	white vinegar	10 mL
	Ice water	

In bowl, combine flour and salt; using pastry blender or two knives, cut in butter and lard until crumbly.

In measuring cup, beat together egg and vinegar; add enough ice water to make 2/3 cup (150 mL) liquid. Stir into flour mixture just until moistened. Shape into 2 rounds; wrap and refrigerate for 1 hour. *(Pastry can be refrigerated for up to 5 days.)* Makes enough for one double-crust or two single crust pies.

Brie and Pecan Tarts

Stretch a package of Brie cheese by baking small wedges topped with a bubbly pecan mixture spiked with whisky or apple juice.

Half	Pastry recipe (this page)	Half
1	pkg (4-1/2 oz/125 g) Brie cheese	1
3 tbsp	finely chopped pecans	50 mL
3 tbsp	packed brown sugar	50 mL
2 tbsp	whisky or apple juice	25 mL

On lightly floured surface, roll out pastry to 1/8-inch (3 mm) thickness; cut out twenty-four 3-inch (8 cm) rounds. Fit into 2-1/4-inch (6 cm) tart tins. Prick each shell in several places with fork. Refrigerate for 30 minutes.

Bake shells in 375°F (190°C) oven for about 20 minutes or until golden. *(Tart shells can be removed from tins, cooled and frozen on baking sheets; store between waxed paper in airtight containers in freezer for up to 2 weeks.)*

Divide Brie into 24 wedges; place each in baked tart shell. In saucepan, heat pecans, sugar and whisky over medium heat, stirring, until bubbly; reduce heat and simmer for 1 minute or until thickened. Working quickly, spoon pecan mixture over Brie. *(Tarts can be covered and refrigerated for up to 1 day; remove from refrigerator 30 minutes before baking.)* Bake in 375°F (190°C) oven for 10 minutes or until hot and bubbly. Makes 24 appetizers.

Chocolate Pecan Pie

Not for calorie-counters, this dessert is definitely over the top in richness.
But then, a little slice is all you need to satisfy a craving.

	Pastry for deep-dish single-crust 10-inch (25 cm) pie (see Perfect Pastry, page 138)	
2 oz	unsweetened chocolate, coarsely chopped	60 g
1/4 cup	butter	50 mL
4	eggs	4
1 cup	packed brown sugar	250 mL
1 cup	corn syrup	250 mL
1-1/2 cups	pecan halves	375 mL
	GARNISH (optional)	
1 oz	semisweet chocolate, melted	30 g
1 oz	white chocolate, melted	30 g

On lightly floured surface, roll out pastry to fit deep 10-inch (25 cm) pie plate; crimp edge. Refrigerate for 30 minutes. (Freeze remaining pastry for another time.)

ᨀ Meanwhile, in small saucepan, heat chocolate with butter over low heat, stirring, for about 1-1/2 minutes or until melted. Let cool slightly.

ᨀ In bowl, whisk eggs with sugar until combined; whisk in corn syrup. Whisk in chocolate mixture.

ᨀ Scatter pecans over pastry shell; pour chocolate mixture over top. Bake on rimmed baking sheet in 375°F (190°C) oven for 40 to 50 minutes or until edge is set but center is still slightly jiggly. Let cool on rack for about 2 hours or until at room temperature. Cover and refrigerate for at least 8 hours or up to 24 hours.

ᨀ GARNISH: If desired, attractively drizzle dark and white chocolate over pie. Makes 12 servings.

Chocolate-Zucchini Cupcakes

Even kids who don't like zucchini will happily eat these treats. Let youngsters have fun decorating the cupcakes with
Easy Chocolate Icing and adding trimmings of colored sprinkles or chopped nuts.

2 oz	unsweetened chocolate	60 g
3	eggs	3
1-3/4 cups	packed brown sugar	425 mL
1 cup	vegetable oil	250 mL
2 cups	all-purpose flour	500 mL
1 tsp	baking powder	5 mL
1 tsp	baking soda	5 mL
1/2 tsp	salt	2 mL
2 cups	finely grated (unpeeled) zucchini (2 small)	500 mL
3/4 cup	finely chopped walnuts or pecans	175 mL
	Easy Chocolate Icing (recipe, page 34)	
	Walnut or pecan halves or colored sprinkles	

In top of double boiler over hot (not boiling) water, melt chocolate. Let cool.

ᨀ In large bowl, beat eggs with sugar for about 10 minutes or until thickened and pale. Blend in oil and cooled chocolate.

ᨀ Stir together flour, baking powder, baking soda and salt; stir into egg mixture just until blended. Stir in zucchini and chopped nuts.

ᨀ Using ice-cream scoop, spoon batter into 24 paper-lined or greased muffin cups, filling two-thirds full. Bake in 350°F (180°C) oven for 20 minutes or until cake tester inserted in center comes out clean. Let cool in pans on rack for 10 minutes. Remove from pans; let cool completely. Spread with Easy Chocolate Icing; garnish with nuts. Makes 24 cupcakes.

Chocolate Dessert Cups

*These prettily fluted cups make an elegant presentation for ice creams, sorbets and rich mousses,
or fresh fruits splashed with liqueur and dolloped with softly whipped cream.*

6 oz	**semisweet chocolate**	175 g

In top of double boiler over hot (not boiling) water, melt chocolate; remove from heat and stir well. Let cool just until soft pudding consistency.

🍃 With small spoon, carefully spread chocolate over inside of 8 fluted paper baking cups, leaving 1/8-inch (3 mm) uncovered border at top. Freeze for 10 to 15 minutes or until hardened; peel off paper. *(Cups can be refrigerated in airtight container for up to 3 days.)* Makes 8 servings.

FLOWERS MAKE IT FESTIVE

A display of flowers adds to any special occasion. Create an artful arrangement from your favorite flowers. Eye-catching displays can be simple yet offer a breathtaking rush of colors, shapes and fragrances.

🍃 Garden flowers impart an informal look. Add greenery from indoor plants like Boston fern or an ivy. Herbs, along with branches and twigs, will fill out the design.

🍃 Garden-grown flowers should be cut in the morning or after sunset. Once indoors, recut flowers and place directly into tepid water treated with floral preservative or a teaspoon of bleach (it keeps the water clean), removing all foliage that will be below the waterline.

🍃 Try to imitate nature — place short flowers like grape hyacinth close to the bottom of the arrangement, taller flowers like daffodils to the back.

THE LITTLE HATTERS' TEA PARTY

"*Wear your garden party best, we'll make hats and then have tea.*" *Dressing up is a wonderful invitation for eight- or nine-year-olds to play "let's pretend." Plain straw hats and trimmings galore greet the partygoers. A mirror propped nearby prompts squeals of delight as each creation takes shape. Adult advice and a helping hand with a glue gun or needle and thread may be required. When the last ribbon is tied and every flower in place, it's time for tea and lots of photos.*

MATERIALS TO SET OUT
🍃 Inexpensive adult-size broad-brimmed straw hats in a choice of colors. Buy these at flea markets, craft stores or discount department stores.

🍃 In advance, you might want to attach a thin round elastic chin strap to each hat.
🍃 Flowers — big and showy, not too delicate.

❧ Sturdy ribbons, preferably 75 to 150 mm wide.

❧ Tulle, cut into strips 75 to 150 mm wide.

❧ White craft glue or a low-melt glue gun (may require adult help).

❧ Pipe cleaners to anchor ribbons or flowers.

❧ Needle and thread.

❧ Self-adhesive Velcro patches are more expensive but easy to use.

TEA PARTY FARE
Old-fashioned tea party sandwiches, tiny cakes and pink "tea" (pink lemonade) in real china cups.

Chapter Three

SUPPER'S
on the
TABLE

"What's for supper?"
*Speedy and delicious, trendy but
friendly, here are dishes guaranteed
to satisfy everyone's cravings.*

Mexican Chicken Dinner

Tex-Mex flavors add zing to simple chicken legs.
Fragrant brown rice and a romaine lettuce salad are perfect
with this main dish. Garnish with lime wedges.

4	chicken legs	4
1/2 tsp	each salt and pepper	2 mL
2 tsp	vegetable oil	10 mL
1	onion, chopped	1
2	cloves garlic, minced	2
2 tsp	chili powder	10 mL
1 tsp	each ground cumin and coriander	5 mL
1/4 tsp	dried oregano	1 mL
Pinch	hot pepper flakes	Pinch
1 tbsp	lime juice	15 mL
2	tomatoes, chopped	2
2	large zucchini, halved lengthwise and thickly sliced	2
1	sweet red or green pepper, chopped	1
2 cups	corn kernels	500 mL
1 cup	shredded Monterey Jack or Cheddar cheese	250 mL

Remove skin from chicken; separate at joint. Sprinkle with half of the salt and pepper.

🍃 In large nonstick ovenproof skillet, heat oil over medium heat; cook chicken, turning once, for about 25 minutes or until golden brown. Transfer to plate.

🍃 Drain off fat from skillet; cook onion and garlic, stirring often, for 3 minutes. Add chili powder, cumin, coriander, oregano, hot pepper flakes and remaining salt and pepper; stir for 30 seconds. Add lime juice, tomatoes, zucchini, red pepper and corn; bring to boil.

🍃 Nestle chicken into vegetable mixture; reduce heat, cover and simmer for 10 to 15 minutes or until vegetables are tender and juices run clear when chicken is pierced. Sprinkle cheese over top; broil for 2 minutes or until cheese is melted and golden. Makes 4 servings.

Microwave Lemon-Herb Chicken and Vegetables

The classic "fines herbes" is a dried mixture of chervil, parsley, chives and tarragon.
You can substitute a mixture of just parsley, chives and tarragon. Serve over noodles or rice.

2 tbsp	butter	25 mL
3	carrots, thinly sliced	3
1	onion, cut into thin wedges	1
1	large clove garlic, minced	1
1 tbsp	liquid honey	15 mL
3/4 tsp	dried fines herbes	4 mL
1/4 tsp	each salt and pepper	1 mL
1 tbsp	water	15 mL
2 tsp	cornstarch	10 mL
1 lb	boneless skinless chicken breasts, cut into 1/2-inch (1 cm) wide strips	500 g
2 cups	small broccoli florets	500 mL
2 tbsp	lemon juice	25 mL

In 12-cup (3 L) microwaveable casserole, microwave butter at High for 30 to 60 seconds or until melted.

ịẻ Add carrots, onion and garlic, stirring to coat well; microwave, uncovered, at High for 3 to 5 minutes or until carrots are tender-crisp, stirring once.

ịẻ Blend in honey, fines herbes, salt and pepper. Combine water with cornstarch; stir into casserole.

ịẻ Add chicken and broccoli, mixing well; cover and microwave at High for 5 to 8 minutes or until chicken is no longer pink inside, stirring twice. Let stand, covered, for 3 minutes. Stir in lemon juice. Makes 4 servings.

Thai-Style Chicken

Here's a smart way to cook once for two meals. A bright balance of flavors offers an exotic
ambience to these juicy chicken breasts, which can be served hot with rice and sugar snap peas or broccoli the first day.
Serve the chicken legs and reserved marinade in a quick Thai Noodle Salad the next day.

1 tbsp	grated lime rind	15 mL
1/3 cup	lime juice	75 mL
1/4 cup	fish sauce	50 mL
3 tbsp	packed brown sugar	50 mL
2 tbsp	ketchup	25 mL
2 tbsp	hoisin sauce	25 mL
1 tbsp	minced gingerroot	15 mL
1 tbsp	chopped jalapeño pepper	15 mL
2	cloves garlic, minced	2
4	each chicken breasts and legs, skinned	4

In large bowl, combine lime rind and juice, fish sauce, sugar, ketchup, hoisin sauce, ginger, jalapeño and garlic. Add chicken, turning to coat; cover and marinate in refrigerator for at least 4 hours or up to 8 hours, turning occasionally. Let stand at room temperature for 30 minutes.

ịẻ Reserving marinade in small saucepan, broil or grill chicken over medium heat for 8 to 12 minutes or until browned, breasts are no longer pink inside and juices run clear when legs are pierced. Meanwhile, bring marinade to boil; boil for 5 minutes.

ịẻ Serve chicken breasts hot. Let marinade and chicken legs cool in refrigerator; cover and store for up to 1 day. Makes 4 servings, plus enough for Thai Noodle Salad.

THAI NOODLE SALAD

Combine marinade and 1/2 tsp (2 mL) sesame oil. Cut meat from chicken legs into bite-size pieces. Toss together marinade, chicken, about 1 lb (500 g) cooked thin pasta, 2 cooked sliced carrots, 1 cup (250 mL) blanched snow peas and 1/4 cup (50 mL) chopped green onion. Makes 4 servings.

Hot Chicken Fajitas

*Fajitas, originally from South America, are a quick sauté of meat —
chicken in this case — and vegetables served in tortillas.*

4	boneless skinless chicken breasts	4
1/4 cup	chicken stock	50 mL
2 tbsp	lime juice	25 mL
2	cloves garlic, minced	2
1 tsp	ground cumin	5 mL
1/2 tsp	ground coriander	2 mL
1/4 tsp	pepper	1 mL
4	large flour tortillas	4
2 tbsp	vegetable oil	25 mL
1	onion, thinly sliced	1
1	small sweet red pepper, cut into thin strips	1
1	hot banana pepper, cut into thin strips	1
	Salt	
	GARNISH	
	Salsa or taco sauce (optional)	
1	tomato, chopped	1
	Sour cream	

Slice chicken crosswise into 1/2-inch (1 cm) wide strips. In large bowl, combine chicken stock, lime juice, garlic, cumin, coriander and pepper; add chicken, stirring to coat. Set aside.

Wrap tortillas in foil; warm in 350°F (180°C) oven for about 10 minutes or until heated through.

Meanwhile, in skillet, heat 1 tbsp (15 mL) of the oil over high heat. Reserving marinade, drain and pat chicken dry. Add chicken to skillet; stir-fry for 4 to 5 minutes or until no longer pink inside. Remove and set aside.

Add remaining oil to skillet; stir-fry onion and red and banana peppers for 1 minute. Pour in reserved marinade; cook, stirring, for 30 seconds or until most of the liquid has evaporated. Return chicken to skillet and heat through. Season with salt to taste.

GARNISH: Spoon salsa (if using) and tomato over each tortilla; top with chicken mixture. Fold up tortillas and garnish filling with dollop of sour cream. Makes 4 servings.

TIP: If a fresh hot banana pepper is unavailable, substitute a few dashes of hot pepper sauce.

Chicken with Peanut Sauce for One

*When you're home alone, this easy peanut sauce with chicken makes a
great dinner for one. Serve over rice or noodles.*

1 tbsp	smooth peanut butter	15 mL
2 tsp	each soy sauce and wine vinegar	10 mL
Pinch	hot pepper flakes	Pinch
1 tsp	vegetable oil	5 mL
1	boneless skinless chicken breast, cut into 1/2-inch (1 cm) cubes	1
2 tsp	minced garlic	10 mL
1 tsp	minced gingerroot	5 mL

In measuring cup, stir together 1/4 cup (50 mL) water, peanut butter, soy sauce, vinegar and hot pepper flakes. In nonstick skillet, heat oil over medium-high heat; cook chicken, garlic and ginger, stirring, for 2 to 3 minutes or until chicken is no longer pink inside.

Stir in peanut butter mixture; bring to boil. Reduce heat to low; cook, stirring, for 3 minutes or until thickened. Makes 1 serving.

FAVORITE FISH TOPPINGS

Delicious fish and fish cakes need a touch of tangy sauce to perk them up. Here's a trio of just such fish toppings.

SALSA MEXICANA

In 2-cup (500 mL) microwaveable measure, combine 1 small onion, finely chopped, 1 clove garlic, minced, and 1 tbsp (15 mL) vegetable oil; microwave at High for 2 minutes or until onion is softened. Stir in 1 cup (250 mL) chopped drained canned tomatoes and 1/4 tsp (1 mL) hot pepper flakes; microwave at High for 3 to 4 minutes or until heated through. Stir in 1 tbsp (15 mL) finely chopped coriander or parsley. Season with salt to taste. Serve hot or cold. Makes 1 cup (250 mL).

MUSTARD-DILL SAUCE

In small saucepan, bring 2/3 cup (150 mL) light cream to boil. Dissolve 1 tbsp (15 mL) cornstarch in 1 tbsp (15 mL) water; whisk into cream and cook, whisking, until thickened and smooth. Stir in 1/3 cup (75 mL) white wine, 1 tbsp (15 mL) chopped fresh dill, and 2 tsp (10 mL) Dijon mustard. Season with salt and pepper to taste. Makes 1 cup (250 mL).

LIGHT TARTAR SAUCE

Combine 2/3 cup (150 mL) plain low-fat yogurt, 1/4 cup (50 mL) relish, 2 tbsp (25 mL) light mayonnaise, 1 tsp (5 mL) each red wine vinegar and Dijon mustard. Makes about 1 cup (250 mL).

Oven-Baked Fish and Chips

Crispy breaded fish and light-style french fries add up to a meal that's economical and delicious.

4	potatoes (about 2 lb/1 kg)	4
2 tbsp	vegetable oil	25 mL
1/2 tsp	salt	2 mL
1/4 tsp	each pepper, dried thyme and rosemary	1 mL

	OVEN-BAKED FISH	
1	pkg (400 g) frozen fish fillets, thawed	1
1/2 cup	all-purpose flour	125 mL
1	egg	1
1/2 cup	dry bread crumbs	125 mL
1/2 cup	cornflake crumbs	125 mL
1/2 tsp	salt	2 mL
1/4 tsp	each dried thyme and pepper	1 mL
1 tbsp	vegetable oil	15 mL

Scrub or peel potatoes; cut into thick french fries and pat dry. Toss with oil, salt, pepper, thyme and rosemary. Arrange in single layer on nonstick baking sheet or foil-lined pan; bake in 425°F (220°C) oven for 40 minutes.

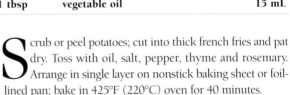 OVEN-BAKED FISH: Meanwhile, cut fish into serving-size pieces; pat dry. Place flour in shallow dish. In another shallow dish, beat egg. In third shallow dish, combine bread crumbs, cornflake crumbs, salt, thyme and pepper.

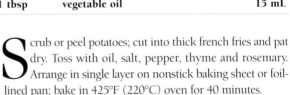 Dip fish into flour to coat. Dip into egg, letting excess drip off. Dip into crumb mixture, patting firmly onto fish.

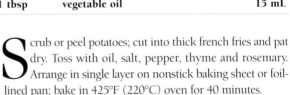 Brush separate baking sheet with oil and arrange fish on sheet; bake, turning once, for 10 minutes or until fish flakes easily when tested with fork and potatoes are tender and golden. Makes 4 servings.

Crispy Fish Cakes

*Bring smiles to young faces at the dinner table with these crunchy
fish-shaped cakes. Carrot and celery eyes and mouths add to the fun. Serve with your favorite
sauce, crisp carrot sticks and broccoli and cauliflower florets.*

1	large baking potato, peeled and quartered	1
1 lb	fish fillets	500 g
1	egg	1
1/4 cup	minced green onion	50 mL
2 tbsp	minced fresh parsley	25 mL
1 tbsp	chopped fresh dill	15 mL
1 tbsp	light mayonnaise	15 mL
1/2 tsp	salt	2 mL
1/4 tsp	pepper	1 mL
Dash	hot pepper sauce	Dash
1/2 cup	dry bread crumbs	125 mL
2 tbsp	vegetable oil	25 mL

In saucepan of boiling salted water, cook potato for 17 to 20 minutes or until tender. Remove with slotted spoon; drain and mash. Set aside.

🐟 In same water, poach fillets over medium-low heat for 5 minutes or until fish flakes easily when tested with fork; drain and process in food processor until smooth.

🐟 In bowl, beat egg; stir in mashed potato, fish, onion, parsley, dill, mayonnaise, salt, pepper and hot pepper sauce. Form into 8 oval patties, 1/2 inch (1 cm) thick. In shallow dish, press patties into bread crumbs to coat all over; press one end into fish-tail shape.

🐟 In large nonstick skillet, heat oil over medium-high heat; cook fish patties for 3 minutes. Using two spatulas, turn fish cakes carefully; cook for 2 to 3 minutes longer or until golden brown. Makes 4 servings.

TIP: In place of fillets, use a can (14.75 oz/418 g) of salmon, drained.

Shepherd's Pie with Three Peppers

Shepherd's Pie can be as simple as meat and potatoes or dressed up with mushrooms and sweet peppers for an added burst of flavor.

4	large potatoes (2 lb/1 kg), peeled and halved	4
3 tbsp	vegetable oil	50 mL
2	onions, chopped	2
1	clove garlic, minced	1
1 cup	sliced mushrooms	250 mL
1 lb	ground beef	500 g
1/2 cup	beef stock	125 mL
1 tbsp	tomato paste	15 mL
1 tbsp	prepared horseradish	15 mL
1 tsp	dry mustard	5 mL
1/2 tsp	dried thyme	2 mL
	Salt and pepper	
1-1/2 cups	diced sweet red, green and yellow peppers	375 mL
1/3 cup	hot milk	75 mL
2	eggs, separated	2
1 cup	shredded Cheddar cheese	250 mL
	Ground nutmeg	

In saucepan of lightly salted boiling water, cook potatoes for about 20 minutes or until tender; drain well.

🍃 Meanwhile, in large skillet, heat 2 tbsp (25 mL) of the oil over medium heat; cook onions and garlic, stirring occasionally, for 5 minutes or until softened. Add mushrooms; cook for 2 to 3 minutes or until golden. Transfer to greased 8-cup (2 L) shallow baking dish; set aside.

🍃 In same skillet, cook beef over medium-high heat, breaking up with back of spoon, for about 5 minutes or until no longer pink. Drain off fat. Add to mushroom mixture.

🍃 In same skillet, bring stock and tomato paste to boil, stirring constantly. Remove from heat. Stir in horseradish, mustard, thyme, 1/2 tsp (2 mL) salt and pinch of pepper; add to meat mixture, mixing well.

🍃 In clean skillet, heat remaining oil over medium heat; cook sweet peppers for 2 to 3 minutes or until tender-crisp. Sprinkle over meat mixture.

🍃 Mash potatoes. Blend in hot milk, egg yolks, Cheddar cheese, 1 tsp (5 mL) salt, and pepper and nutmeg to taste. Beat egg whites until stiff peaks form; fold into potato mixture. Spoon evenly over meat mixture.

🍃 Bake in 425°F (220°C) oven for 15 minutes. Reduce heat to 350°F (180°C); bake for 20 minutes longer or until filling is bubbly and top is golden. Makes 6 servings.

TIP: When the price of red and yellow peppers is high, use 1 cup (250 mL) green pepper only. A bit of color is lost but the flavor is the same.

Mini Meat Loaf Muffins

Meat loaf is a comfort food we can all identify with. For this fast meal, we used muffin tins instead of a small loaf pan.

1	egg	1
1/4 cup	dry bread crumbs	50 mL
1-1/2 tsp	dried basil	7 mL
1 tsp	Dijon mustard	5 mL
1/2 tsp	salt	2 mL
1/4 tsp	pepper	1 mL
1 lb	lean ground beef	500 g
2	green onions, chopped	2
1	carrot, shredded	1
3 tbsp	chili sauce	50 mL

In bowl, beat egg; mix in bread crumbs, basil, mustard, salt and pepper. Mix in beef, onions and carrot; form into 6 balls.

🍃 Place meatballs in muffin tins; top with chili sauce. Bake in 375°F (190°C) oven for 20 to 25 minutes or until no longer pink inside. Makes 4 servings.

Saucy Meatball Pockets

*Top these family-pleasing meatballs with chopped
cucumber and tomatoes, and sour cream or yogurt.*

1	egg	1
1-1/2 lb	lean ground beef	750 g
1/2 cup	minced green onion	125 mL
1 tsp	dried mint	5 mL
3/4 tsp	dried oregano	4 mL
1/2 tsp	salt	2 mL
1/4 tsp	pepper	1 mL
4 tsp	vegetable oil	20 mL
1	sweet red pepper, cut into bite-size chunks	1
1 cup	ketchup	250 mL
1/2 tsp	Worcestershire sauce	2 mL
3	pitas, halved	3
	Crinkle-Cut Oven Fries (recipe follows)	

In bowl, lightly beat egg; mix in beef, onion, mint, oregano, salt and pepper. Shape into 18 meatballs. Set aside.

🍃 In large skillet, heat 1 tsp (5 mL) of the oil over medium-high heat; cook red pepper, stirring, for 3 to 5 minutes or until softened. Remove and set aside.

🍃 In same skillet, heat remaining oil; cook meatballs for 5 minutes or until browned all over. Reduce heat to medium; cover and cook, stirring occasionally, for 8 to 10 minutes or until no longer pink inside. Drain off fat.

🍃 Combine ketchup and Worcestershire sauce; add to skillet and cook, stirring, for about 3 minutes or until meatballs are coated.

🍃 Spoon 3 meatballs, some red pepper and heaping tablespoonful (15 mL) sauce into each pita half. Serve with Crinkle-Cut Oven Fries. Makes 6 servings.

CRINKLE-CUT OVEN FRIES

3	baking potatoes, peeled	3
3 tbsp	vegetable oil	50 mL
	Salt and pepper	

🍃 Using crinkle-edged cutter or garnishing knife, slice potatoes 1/4 inch (5 mm) thick. Place on greased broiler rack; brush with half of the oil. Season with salt and pepper to taste. Broil for 8 minutes. Turn and brush with remaining oil; broil for 4 to 5 minutes or until crisp. Makes 6 servings.

Classic Lasagna

A triple-layer lasagna may take a little time to assemble, but the compliments from family and friends make it well worth the effort. Choose plain, spinach, tomato or whole wheat noodles for variety in this dish.

3/4 lb	lasagna noodles	375 g
2 tbsp	freshly grated Parmesan cheese	25 mL
	CHEESE FILLING	
3 cups	trimmed fresh spinach	750 mL
3/4 lb	ricotta cheese	375 g
1	egg, beaten	1
2 tbsp	each chopped fresh basil and chives	25 mL
1 cup	Béchamel Sauce (recipe follows)	250 mL
	MEAT SAUCE	
1/3 lb	lean ground beef	170 g
1 cup	sliced mushrooms	250 mL
1	onion, chopped	1
1	clove garlic, minced	1
1 cup	tomato sauce	250 mL
1/2 tsp	salt	2 mL
	Pepper	

CHEESE FILLING: Rinse spinach under water; shake off excess. In saucepan, cover spinach and cook, with just the water clinging to leaves, over medium-high heat for about 5 minutes or just until wilted. Drain well and squeeze dry; chop and place in bowl. Stir in ricotta, egg, basil and chives. Stir in 3/4 cup (175 mL) of the Béchamel Sauce. Set aside.

🍴 MEAT SAUCE: In skillet, cook beef, mushrooms, onion and garlic over medium-high heat, breaking up meat with back of spoon, for about 5 minutes or until meat is no longer pink. Drain off any fat. Add tomato sauce, salt, and pepper to taste; simmer for 10 minutes.

🍴 Meanwhile, in large pot of boiling salted water, cook noodles for 6 to 8 minutes or until almost tender. Drain and cool in cold water; drain well and arrange in single layer on damp tea towel.

🍴 Arrange one-quarter of the noodles over bottom of lightly greased 12- x 8-inch (3 L) baking dish; cover with half of the cheese filling. Top with second layer of noodles; cover with meat sauce. Add another layer of noodles, remaining cheese filling and final layer of noodles. Spread with remaining Béchamel Sauce; sprinkle with Parmesan.

🍴 Bake in 350°F (180°C) oven for 40 to 50 minutes or until lightly browned and bubbly. Let stand for 10 minutes. Makes about 8 servings.

	BÉCHAMEL SAUCE	
2 tbsp	butter	25 mL
2 tbsp	all-purpose flour	25 mL
1/4 tsp	salt	1 mL
	Pepper	
1 cup	milk	250 mL

🍴 In small saucepan, melt butter over medium heat. Blend in flour, salt, and pepper to taste; cook, whisking, for 1 minute. Gradually whisk in milk; cook, whisking, until boiling and thickened. Makes 1 cup (250 mL).

MAKING WAVES

Here are some easy everyday microwave shortcuts that make a great kitchen helper even greater.

❧ SOFTEN BUTTER OR CREAM CHEESE: Microwave 1/2 cup (125 mL) at Medium-Low (30%) for 20 to 40 seconds or until softened.

❧ TOAST NUTS AND COCONUT: Spread 1/2 cup (125 mL) evenly on microwaveable glass pie plate. Microwave at High for 2 to 4 minutes or just until lightly toasted, stirring often.

❧ MELT CHOCOLATE: Microwave 1 oz (30 g) chocolate at Medium (50%) for 2 minutes or until melted, stirring occasionally. Microwave 1/2 lb (250 g) chopped chocolate at Medium (50%) for 6 to 8 minutes, stirring occasionally.

❧ CLARIFY BUTTER: Place 1/2 cup (125 mL) butter in 2-cup (500 mL) measure. Microwave at High for 1-1/2 to 2 minutes or until boiling. Remove from microwave; skim froth from top. Let stand until separated. The clear top layer is clarified butter. Discard milk solids left at bottom.

❧ SOFTEN SQUASH FOR EASY CUTTING: Microwave pierced whole squash at High for 2 to 3 minutes.

❧ DISSOLVE UNFLAVORED GELATIN: Sprinkle gelatin over the liquid as specified in recipe. Let stand for 1 minute; microwave at Medium (50%) for 30 to 60 seconds or until gelatin has dissolved.

❧ DRY HERBS: Place 1/2 cup (125 mL) fresh parsley, basil, tarragon, sage or oregano leaves between 2 sheets of paper towelling. Microwave at High for 1-1/2 to 2-1/2 minutes, or until crumbly, stirring once.

❧ SOFTEN BROWN SUGAR: In bowl, top 1 cup (250 mL) hard brown sugar with a slice of bread or piece of apple; cover with small piece of waxed paper. Cover and microwave at High for 30 to 60 seconds or until brown sugar is softened. Let stand for 5 minutes.

❧ MAKE CROUTONS: Place 2 cups (500 mL) bread cubes in single layer in shallow dish. Microwave at High for 3 to 4 minutes or until crisp, stirring once.

❧ GET MORE JUICE FROM CITRUS FRUIT: Microwave 1 whole orange, lemon or lime at High for 30 seconds. Cut and squeeze.

Microwave Beef-Topped Tostadas

Crispy tortillas topped with a spicy Mexican-flavored beef are a snap to make. Serve these microwaved tostadas open-faced with sour cream or salsa.

4	large flour tortillas	4
1 lb	lean ground beef	500 g
1	onion, chopped	1
1	jalapeño pepper, seeded and diced	1
1	clove garlic, minced	1
1 tbsp	chili powder	15 mL
1 tsp	ground cumin	5 mL
1/4 tsp	salt	1 mL
Pinch	pepper	Pinch
1	large tomato, seeded and chopped	1
1 cup	each shredded lettuce and Cheddar cheese	250 mL

Pierce tortillas in a few places; microwave each on microwaveable rack at High for 1-1/2 to 2 minutes or until barely crisp, turning and rotating once. Place on microwaveable plates.

❧ In 8-cup (2 L) microwaveable bowl, crumble beef. Add onion, jalapeño and garlic; microwave at High, stirring often, for 3 to 5 minutes or until meat is no longer pink. Stir in chili powder, cumin, salt and pepper. Add tomato; microwave at High for 1 to 2 minutes or until hot.

❧ Using slotted spoon, divide beef mixture among tortillas; sprinkle with lettuce, then Cheddar cheese. Microwave each at High for 30 to 60 seconds or until cheese melts. Makes 4 servings.

Beef and Vegetable Stir-Fry with Noodles

*Stir-fries are a fast and easy way to serve up a meal. Oriental-style
vegetables are readily available at your supermarket.*

3 tbsp	each wine vinegar and soy sauce	50 mL
2 tbsp	packed brown sugar	25 mL
1 tbsp	cornstarch	15 mL
1 lb	round steak	500 mL
2 tbsp	vegetable oil	25 mL
1	pkg (750 g) frozen Oriental-style mixed vegetables	1
1	pkg (350 g) steamed Chinese noodles, broken up	1

I n small bowl, combine vinegar, soy sauce, sugar, cornstarch and 2 tbsp (25 mL) water; stir until cornstarch is dissolved. Set aside.

🍃 Trim fat from steak; cut meat into thin slices diagonally. In nonstick skillet or large wok, heat half of the oil over medium-high heat; cook meat, stirring, for 2 to 3 minutes or until well browned. Remove and set aside.

🍃 Add remaining oil to pan; stir-fry vegetables for 5 to 6 minutes or until tender. Stir cornstarch mixture; stir into pan along with meat. Cook, stirring, until sauce is boiling and thickened. Add noodles; cook until heated through. Makes 4 servings.

Stir-Fried Chicken with Snow Peas and Cherry Tomatoes

This Chinese-style dish has a full fresh flavor and colorful appearance. Serve over steamed rice or noodles.

1-1/2 lb	boneless, skinless chicken breasts	750 g
1 tbsp	cornstarch	15 mL
1 tbsp	rice wine	15 mL
1 tbsp	soy sauce	15 mL
1	egg white, lightly beaten	1
1/3 cup	peanut or corn oil	75 mL
2	cloves garlic, minced	2
1 tbsp	chopped gingerroot	15 mL
2	green onions, chopped	2
3/4 lb	snow peas	375 g
2 cups	cherry tomatoes	500 mL
	Salt	
	SAUCE	
1/2 cup	chicken stock	125 mL
2 tbsp	soy sauce	25 mL
1 tbsp	rice wine	15 mL
2 tsp	cornstarch	10 mL
1 tsp	sesame oil	5 mL

Cut chicken into 1-1/2-inch (4 cm) cubes. In bowl, combine cornstarch, rice wine, soy sauce and egg white; add chicken. Let marinate at room temperature for 20 minutes.

✿ SAUCE: Combine stock, soy sauce, rice wine, cornstarch and sesame oil; set aside.

✿ In wok or skillet, heat 3 tbsp (50 mL) of the oil over high heat; stir-fry chicken until no longer pink inside. Remove and set aside. Wipe out wok.

✿ Heat remaining oil in wok; stir-fry garlic, ginger and onions for 1 minute or until fragrant. Add snow peas; stir-fry for 1 minute. Add tomatoes and reserved chicken; stir-fry for 1 minute.

✿ Stir sauce and pour into wok; cook, stirring constantly, until boiling and thickened. Season with salt to taste. Makes 4 to 6 servings.

WOK TALK: A STIR-FRYING GUIDE

Easy, fast wok cooking is a dramatic one-pot cooking style. Even without a wok, a simple heavy skillet cooks colorful vegetables just enough to retain a flavorful crunch.

✿ Stir-frying is not as frantic as it often looks. Read the recipe through before starting, then prepare the ingredients and set them out in small bowls by the stove.

A BASIC STIR-FRY GOES LIKE THIS:

✿ To hot oil, add a garlic-ginger mixture; cook just until fragrant.

✿ Add meat (if using) a little at a time and cook until no longer pink. Remove as browned. (If you add too much at once, the meat steams instead of browning.)

✿ Add onion and other vegetables and stir-fry for 1 or 2 minutes.

✿ Add chicken stock; cover and steam vegetables until tender-crisp.

✿ Return meat to veggie mixture and stir in a flavoring sauce, usually soy sauce, oyster sauce, cornstarch, sherry or vinegar, sugar and chili paste. Toss everything together until meat and vegetables are glazed.

✿ Serve at once over rice or noodles.

COOKING PERFECT RICE

✿ Bring 1-1/3 cups (325 mL) water to boil. Stir in 2/3 cup (150 mL) parboiled, brown or whole grain rice and pinch of salt.

✿ Cover and reduce heat; simmer parboiled rice for 20 minutes, brown rice for 40 minutes, or whole grain rice for 25 minutes, or until rice is tender and liquid absorbed. Makes 2 cups (500 mL) cooked rice, enough for 4 servings.

Mustard-Basil Sausages

*Farmer's sausages fit the grilling bill. Watch them brown and crisp
on the barbecue, yet stay juicy inside, thanks to precooking beforehand. Serve with
applesauce, yogurt-topped barbecued or baked potatoes, spinach and pickled beets.*

2 lb	farmer's sausage	1 kg
1/4 cup	prepared mustard	50 mL
2 tbsp	liquid honey	25 mL
1/2 tsp	dried basil	2 mL

In large skillet, cover sausage with water; bring to boil. Reduce heat to medium-low; cover and simmer for 12 minutes. Drain well; cut into thirds.

❧ In bowl, stir together mustard, honey and basil.

❧ Place sausage on greased grill over medium-high heat; cook, turning often, for 5 minutes. Cook, brushing with mustard mixture, for 5 minutes longer. Makes 6 servings.

Hoisin Ribs

*Simmer the ribs before grilling and ensure juicy, tender results.
Serve with a medley of grilled vegetables such as potatoes,
red peppers and zucchini or a fresh green salad.*

4 lb	pork side ribs	2 kg	1 tbsp	marmalade or liquid honey	15 mL
1/2 cup	hoisin sauce	125 mL	1 tsp	minced gingerroot	5 mL
3 tbsp	white wine vinegar	50 mL	1 tsp	sesame oil	5 mL
3 tbsp	soy sauce	50 mL	1	clove garlic, minced	1
			2	green onions, chopped	2

Cut ribs into four serving-size portions; place in large heavy saucepan. Pour in just enough water to cover ribs; bring to boil. Reduce heat to low; cover and simmer for 45 minutes or until tender. Drain.

❧ In small bowl, combine hoisin sauce, vinegar, soy sauce, marmalade, ginger, sesame oil and garlic.

❧ Place ribs on greased grill over medium heat; cook, turning often and brushing with sauce, for 12 to 15 minutes or until well coated and browned. Serve sprinkled with green onions. Makes 4 servings.

Orange Pork Chops

For a fast supper treat or delicious company fare, these easy chops are the answer.
Dress them up with a splash of wine.

1 tbsp	chopped fresh parsley	15 mL
1/4 tsp	fennel seeds, crushed	1 mL
1	clove garlic, crushed	1
	Salt and pepper	
4	center-cut pork chops, trimmed	4
2 tbsp	vegetable oil	25 mL
2 tsp	cornstarch	10 mL
3/4 cup	orange juice	175 mL
	Orange slices	

Combine parsley, fennel seeds, garlic and 1/4 tsp (1 mL) each salt and pepper; rub all over pork chops.
❧ In skillet, heat oil over medium-high heat; cook chops for 2 to 3 minutes per side or just until no longer pink inside. Remove to platter and keep warm.
❧ Pour off fat in skillet. Dissolve cornstarch in 1 tbsp (15 mL) of the orange juice; stir back into remaining orange juice. Pour into skillet and cook, stirring, for 2 minutes or until boiling and thickened. Season with salt and pepper to taste. Pour over chops; garnish with orange slices. Makes 4 servings.

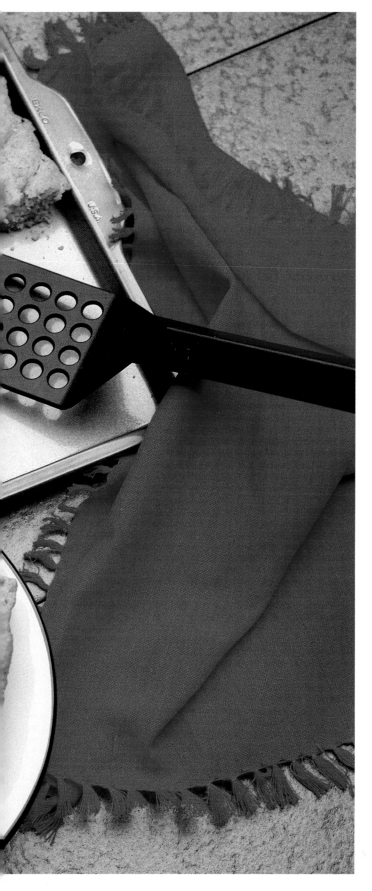

Quick Whole Wheat Pizza

Who doesn't like pizza? For a speedy pizza base, use this nutritious, delicious biscuit-type crust.

1-1/2 cups	whole wheat flour	375 mL
1 cup	all-purpose flour	250 mL
1 cup	cornmeal	250 mL
2 tsp	baking powder	10 mL
1 tsp	baking soda	5 mL
1 tsp	salt	5 mL
1-1/2 cups	plain low-fat yogurt	375 mL
1/4 cup	canola oil	50 mL
	TOPPING	
2	cans (each 19 oz/540 mL) Italian Spice stewed tomatoes	2
2 cups	broccoli florets	500 mL
1 cup	thinly sliced carrots	250 mL
1-1/2 cups	shredded low-fat mozzarella cheese	375 mL
	Salt and pepper	
1	sweet green pepper, chopped	1
1/4 cup	freshly grated Parmesan cheese	50 mL

In large bowl, combine whole wheat and all-purpose flours, cornmeal, baking powder, baking soda and salt. Combine yogurt and oil; pour over flour mixture and stir with fork to combine. On lightly floured surface, knead dough lightly into ball. *(Dough can be covered and refrigerated for up to 8 hours.)*

&• With dampened hands, press dough into greased 15- x 10-inch (40 x 25 cm) jelly roll pan. Bake in 400°F (200°C) oven for 10 to 12 minutes or until firm.

&• TOPPING: Meanwhile, drain and chop tomatoes, reserving juice for other use; return to sieve and set aside to drain.

&• Meanwhile, in saucepan of boiling water, cook broccoli and carrots for 2 to 3 minutes or until partially cooked but still crunchy. Drain and refresh under cold water.

&• Sprinkle half of the mozzarella cheese over crust. Sprinkle tomatoes over cheese. Sprinkle with salt and pepper to taste. Top with broccoli, carrots and green pepper; sprinkle with remaining mozzarella and Parmesan cheese. Bake for 15 to 20 minutes or until bottom of crust is golden. Makes 8 servings.

TIP: If Italian Spice stewed tomatoes are unavailable, substitute regular stewed tomatoes and 1/2 tsp (2 mL) dried basil.

Green Vegetable Risotto

*Serve this light version of risotto — flecked with vegetables,
bursting with flavor, but low in fat — as a vegetarian main dish. Or team it with chicken,
a green salad and whole-grain bread for a satisfying supper.*

2 tbsp	butter	25 mL
1/2 cup	sliced green onions	125 mL
1 cup	Italian Arborio or short grain rice	250 mL
4 cups	simmering chicken stock	1 L
1 cup	sliced green beans	250 mL
12	snow peas	12
1 cup	coarsely chopped zucchini	250 mL
1/4 cup	chopped fresh parsley	50 mL
1/4 cup	freshly grated Parmesan cheese	50 mL
	Pepper	

In large nonstick skillet, melt half of the butter over medium heat; cook onions, stirring, for about 1 minute or until softened. Add rice, stirring to coat.

Add half of the chicken stock, 1/4 cup (50 mL) at a time, cooking and stirring until each addition is absorbed before adding next, about 8 minutes in total.

Stir in green beans; cook for 2 minutes. Stir in snow peas and zucchini.

Stir in remaining stock, 1/4 cup (50 mL) at a time, cooking and stirring until each addition is absorbed before adding next or until rice is creamy but still firm, 10 to 15 minutes in total. Stir in parsley, Parmesan, remaining butter, and pepper to taste. Makes 4 servings.

Mediterranean Vegetable Stew

Bring home the exciting flavors and textures of the Mediterranean with this couscous vegetable stew.

1 tbsp	vegetable oil	15 mL
1	large onion, chopped	1
2	stalks celery, sliced	2
2 cups	cubed peeled rutabaga or turnip	500 mL
2	large carrots, thinly sliced	2
1	can (28 oz/796 mL) tomatoes	1
1	can (19 oz/540 mL) chick-peas, drained and rinsed	1
1	zucchini, sliced	1
1	sweet green pepper, sliced	1
1 tsp	ground cumin	5 mL
1/4 tsp	ground coriander	1 mL
1/4 tsp	hot pepper flakes	1 mL
	Salt and pepper	
2-2/3 cups	water	650 mL
1-1/2 cups	couscous	375 mL
	Chopped fresh coriander or parsley	

In large nonstick saucepan, heat oil over medium heat; cook onion, stirring occasionally, for 5 minutes or until softened. Add celery, rutabaga and carrots; cook for 5 minutes, stirring occasionally.

Add tomatoes, breaking up with back of spoon; bring to boil. Reduce heat, cover and simmer for 20 minutes or until rutabaga is tender-crisp.

Add chick-peas, zucchini, green pepper, cumin, ground coriander, hot pepper flakes, and salt and pepper to taste; simmer for 10 minutes or until zucchini is tender. (*Stew can be cooled in refrigerator, covered and stored for up to 1 day; reheat to serve.*)

Meanwhile, in another saucepan, bring water to boil; stir in couscous. Cover and remove from heat; let stand for 5 minutes. Fluff with fork.

Serve stew over couscous; sprinkle with fresh coriander. Makes 6 servings.

TIPS: Couscous, sometimes called Moroccan pasta, is available in most supermarkets in a packaged variety that is ready in five minutes. If you can't find it, substitute cooked brown rice.

Other vegetables, such as squash or frozen peas, can also be used.

Microwave Savory Onion and Cheese Bake

A microwave makes this a quick light supper or brunch dish. Serve with a salad or steamed broccoli.

3	onions	3
1 tbsp	butter	15 mL
1 cup	milk	250 mL
3	eggs	3
1/4 tsp	dried basil	1 mL
Pinch	each salt and pepper	Pinch
2 cups	shredded Cheddar cheese (1/2 lb/250 g)	500 mL
1-1/2 cups	fresh whole wheat bread crumbs	375 mL
1	tomato, seeded and chopped	1

Cut onions in half lengthwise; slice thinly. In 9-inch (23 cm) microwaveable quiche dish, deep-dish pie plate or round cake pan, microwave butter at High for 30 to 60 seconds or until melted; stir in onions to coat well. Cover and microwave at High for 5 to 8 minutes or until softened and translucent, stirring twice. Let stand, covered.

Meanwhile, in 1-cup (250 mL) microwaveable measure, microwave milk at High for 2 to 3 minutes or until hot but not boiling, stirring once. In bowl, lightly whisk eggs; gradually whisk in milk, then basil, salt and pepper. Stir in cheese and bread crumbs.

Sprinkle tomato evenly over onions; pour egg mixture over top. Microwave, uncovered, at Medium-High (70%) for 10 to 14 minutes or until set in center, rotating once. Cover and let stand directly on counter for 10 minutes before serving. Makes 4 servings.

Chapter Four

KIDS COOK IT UP

"You're never too young to learn!" From all-time winners such as buttermilk pancakes to pizza to share with pals, here are recipes for all ages and stages.

Quick-Mixing Pizza Dough

Here's a quick pizza dough that kids will just love to get their hands into.

2-1/2 cups	all-purpose flour	625 mL
1	pkg quick-rising (instant) dry yeast (or 1 tbsp/15 mL)	1
1 tsp	salt	5 mL
1 cup	hot water	250 mL
2 tbsp	vegetable oil	25 mL

In large bowl, combine 1-1/2 cups (375 mL) of the flour, yeast and salt. Pour hot (not boiling) water and oil into flour mixture; mix well. Mix in remaining flour to make slightly sticky dough. Form into ball.

❧ On lightly floured surface, knead dough for about 5 minutes or until smooth and elastic. Cut dough in half; cover and let rest for 10 minutes. On lightly floured surface, roll out each half into 12-inch (30 cm) diameter circle.

❧ Transfer to 2 lightly greased 12-inch (30 cm) pizza pans or baking sheets. Carefully stretch and pull dough to fit pans; let rise for about 15 minutes before adding toppings. (For slightly thicker crust, let dough rise for about 30 minutes.) Makes two 12-inch (30 cm) unbaked pizza bases.

VARIATION
❧ WHOLE WHEAT PIZZA DOUGH: Use 1-1/2 cups (375 mL) all-purpose flour and 1 cup (250 mL) whole wheat flour.

KID-PLEASING TOPPINGS

After spreading the pizza round with a spicy tomato sauce, try several of the following:
- ❧ *sliced tomatoes*
- ❧ *chopped green and yellow sweet peppers*
- ❧ *chopped black or green olives*
- ❧ *sliced artichoke hearts*
- ❧ *sliced mushrooms*
- ❧ *anchovies or drained flaked tuna*
- ❧ *chopped ham, crumbled cooked bacon, sliced pepperoni*
- ❧ *grated Parmesan or shredded mozzarella or Monterey Jack cheese*
- ❧ *crumbled dried oregano and basil*

SIX STEPS TO THE PERFECT PIZZA

1. Fold dough in half.

2. Push dough away with heels of hands.

3. Give dough a quarter turn and repeat.

4. Stretch dough to fit pan.

5. Cover with tomato sauce.

6. Add all the toppings.

Cheese and Pepperoni Pizza

This is a very simple, basic pizza. For additional topping suggestions, see box on page 68.

1	can (14 oz/398 mL) tomato sauce	1
1 tsp	each crumbled dried oregano and basil	5 mL
2	cloves garlic, minced	2
2	unbaked 12-inch (30 cm) pizza bases (see Quick-Mixing Pizza Dough, page 68)	2
3 cups	shredded mozzarella cheese	750 mL
1 cup	thinly sliced pepperoni	250 mL

Combine tomato sauce, oregano, basil and garlic; spread over pizza bases. Sprinkle with cheese; arrange pepperoni over top.

✷ Bake in lower half of 450°F (230°C) oven for 16 to 18 minutes or until crust is golden brown and cheese is bubbly. Makes 2 pizzas.

Tuna Sandwiches

Making something simple and well-loved is often the best way to begin your cooking career.
Even an uncomplicated sandwich needs care and a guiding hand to show little cooks the right way.

1	stalk celery, finely chopped	1
1	can (184 g) flaked white tuna, drained	1
2 tbsp	mayonnaise	25 mL
1 tbsp	relish	15 mL
6	slices whole wheat bread	6
3	lettuce leaves	3

In bowl, combine celery, tuna, mayonnaise and relish; spread over 3 of the bread slices. Top with lettuce and remaining bread, pressing down gently. Cut in half. Makes 3 servings.

Croque-Monsieur

With supervision, even young children can make this tasty version of a grilled cheese sandwich.

2 tbsp	butter, softened	25 mL
4	slices whole wheat or white bread	4
4	thin slices mild Cheddar or Swiss cheese	4
2	thin slices cooked ham or chicken	2

Butter bread slices on one side. Top unbuttered side of 2 slices with half of the cheese, the ham, then remaining cheese. Top with remaining bread, buttered side up; press lightly.

✷ In skillet, cook sandwiches over medium heat, turning once, for 6 to 8 minutes or until golden and cheese has melted. Cut diagonally in half. Makes 2 servings.

Plum Cheese Spread

Often the food you make as a child is the best. So let kids pipe this mixture onto their own crackers or carrot and cucumber rounds, or even into celery sticks.

1/2 lb	cream cheese	250 g
1/2 cup	shredded mild Cheddar cheese	125 mL
2 tbsp	mayonnaise or plain yogurt	25 mL
2 tbsp	plum sauce	25 mL

In food processor or blender, beat together cream cheese and Cheddar until smooth. Add mayonnaise and plum sauce; purée until smooth. Makes about 1-1/4 cups (300 mL).

Orange-Glazed Chicken Wings

Although an adult should help to cut up the wings, young children can mix the glaze, which is also good on chicken thighs or drumsticks.

2-3/4 lb	chicken wings (about 16)	1.4 kg
1/4 tsp	each salt and pepper	1 mL
	GLAZE	
1/4 cup	frozen orange juice concentrate, thawed	50 mL
3 tbsp	liquid honey	50 mL
1 tbsp	soy sauce	15 mL
1/4 tsp	ground ginger	1 mL

1	clove garlic, minced	1
Dash	Worcestershire sauce	Dash
Pinch	salt	Pinch

Separate chicken wings at joint; cut off and discard wing tips. Place wings on greased foil-lined baking sheet. Sprinkle with salt and pepper. Bake in 400°F (200°C) oven for 30 minutes, turning once.

☙ GLAZE: Combine orange juice concentrate, honey, soy sauce, ginger, garlic, Worcestershire sauce and salt; brush over wings. Bake for 10 minutes longer or until browned, crisp and no longer pink inside. Makes 4 servings.

Veggie Platter with Dip

Young children can blend ingredients for this dip while older siblings prepare their favorite raw vegetables. Carrot sticks, cauliflower and broccoli florets, sticks of celery, zucchini and peppers, as well as cherry tomatoes and cucumber rounds make a colorful platter to serve at a barbecue or for a healthy TV snack.

1 cup	creamed cottage cheese	250 mL
1/3 cup	sour cream or plain yogurt	75 mL
2 tbsp	finely chopped fresh parsley	25 mL
2 tbsp	finely chopped green onion	25 mL
1 tsp	Dijon mustard	5 mL
	Salt and pepper	
6 cups	raw vegetable sticks or chunks	1.5 L

In blender or food processor, beat together cottage cheese and sour cream until smooth; spoon into bowl. Stir in parsley, green onion, mustard, and salt and pepper to taste. Place in center of large platter; surround with raw vegetables. Makes 6 servings.

A PRIMER FOR FIRST-TIME COOKS

BEFORE YOU BEGIN

&. *Ask permission. Sometimes help is really appreciated. Other times it's just not a good time for kids in the kitchen.*

&. *Put on an apron and wash your hands with soap and water.*

&. *Read through the recipe; get out all the ingredients and equipment called for.*

&. *Ask an adult for help if you're unsure of the step or if you have to use the stove, oven, blender or food processor, chop with sharp knives, or drain boiling water.*

&. *Have a cloth handy to wipe up any spills.*

WORKING NEAR THE STOVE

&. *Be sure you know how to turn the elements on and off, and how to increase or lower the heat.*

&. *Turn pot handles to the side, away from the front of the stove, to prevent accidents.*

&. *To stir food in a saucepan, hold the handle firmly and use a wooden spoon or one with a wooden or plastic handle that won't get too hot.*

&. *Keep pot holders or oven mitts handy. Use them for removing anything from the oven. Set hot pans on trivets or a wooden board — not directly on the counter.*

&. *Be sure hands are dry when plugging in (or unplugging) electric appliances. To unplug, grasp the plug — don't just pull the cord.*

MEASURING

&. *Careful measuring gives best results. Use either the imperial measures or the metric measures in a recipe but don't switch back and forth.*

&. *When measuring dry ingredients in measuring spoons or dry measure cups, fill the measure and level off with the straight edge of a knife.*

&. *When measuring a liquid, use a clear measuring cup. Set it on a flat surface and fill to the level you need, bending down so your eyes are even with the cup.*

TIDY UP

&. *Try to leave the kitchen as neat as you found it.*

&. *Put away ingredients such as butter, milk, sugar, as you finish with them.*

&. *Rinse dishes as you go; they'll be easier to wash later.*

Microwave Herbed Potato Sticks

Today's kids are comfortable with microwave cooking. Let them pitch in with
dinner by making these seasoned potato sticks.

1/4 cup	finely chopped onion	50 mL
2 tbsp	olive oil	25 mL
1 tbsp	butter	15 mL
1	clove garlic, minced	1
3 tbsp	chopped fresh parsley	50 mL
1 tbsp	chopped fresh basil (or 1/2 tsp/2 mL dried)	15 mL
1 tsp	chili powder	5 mL
1/4 tsp	salt	1 mL
Pinch	pepper	Pinch
4	large potatoes, scrubbed	4

In 8-cup (2 L) microwaveable baking dish, combine onion, oil, butter and garlic; microwave at High for 1-1/2 to 2 minutes or until onion is softened, stirring once. Stir in parsley, basil, chili powder, salt and pepper. Set aside.

❧ Halve potatoes lengthwise; cut each half into 4 sticks. Add to baking dish; toss to coat evenly. Cover and microwave at High for 10 to 12 minutes or until fork-tender, stirring halfway through. To serve, spoon onion mixture over potatoes. Makes 4 servings.

MICROWAVE SAFETY RULES FOR KIDS

Please be sure that children are familiar with the careful use of microwave ovens.

❧ *Never turn on an empty oven.*

❧ *Keep oven mitts handy. While micro-cooking is cool cooking, food and dishes can get very hot.*

❧ *As you uncover cooked food, lift the lid or plastic wrap away from you to prevent steam burns.*

❧ *Never use metal cookware, metal twist ties, gold or silver-trimmed china or conventional meat or candy thermometers in the microwave. Use only microwaveable bowls and utensils.*

❧ *If you hear popping or sputtering noises, open the oven door and check. A simple rearranging or turning may solve the problem.*

❧ *Never try to cook eggs in their shell.*

❧ *Never try to pop popping corn in a brown paper bag.*

Wonton Soup

Children love to wrap the dumplings that go into this soup. Fresh or frozen wonton wrappers are available in Chinese grocery stores and most supermarkets.

6 cups	chicken stock	1.5 L
1 tbsp	soy sauce	15 mL
1	carrot, thinly sliced on diagonal	1
12	snow peas, halved diagonally	12
	Salt	
	WONTONS	
1/4 lb	ground chicken	125 g
1 tsp	soy sauce	5 mL
1 tsp	cornstarch	5 mL
1/2 tsp	salt	2 mL
1/2 tsp	sesame oil	2 mL

1 tbsp	chopped carrot	15 mL
1 tbsp	chopped chives or green onion	15 mL
24	wonton wrappers	24

WONTONS: In bowl, combine chicken, soy sauce, cornstarch, salt and oil; stir in carrot and chives. Spoon 1 tsp (5 mL) onto each wonton wrapper; bring edges up around filling to resemble little pouches, squeezing to seal.

In large saucepan, bring stock, soy sauce and carrot to boil; reduce heat and simmer for 5 minutes. Add wontons; cook for 3 minutes or until filling is no longer pink and wrappers are tender. Add snow peas; cook for 30 seconds. Season with salt to taste. Makes 6 servings.

Vegetable Burritos with Winter Salsa

These spicy burritos are nutritious as well as delicious.

1 tsp	vegetable oil	5 mL
2	onions, chopped	2
1	clove garlic, minced	1
1	sweet green pepper, chopped	1
1 cup	finely diced zucchini	250 mL
1	large carrot, grated	1
2 tsp	chili powder	10 mL
1 tsp	each dried oregano and ground cumin	5 mL
	Salt and pepper	
1-1/2 cups	Winter Salsa (recipe follows)	375 mL
1	can (14 oz/398 mL) refried beans	1
5	9-inch (23 cm) flour tortillas	5
1/2 cup	shredded Cheddar cheese	125 mL
1/2 cup	plain low-fat yogurt	125 mL

In nonstick skillet, heat oil over medium heat; cook onions, stirring occasionally, for 3 minutes. Add garlic, green pepper, zucchini and carrot; cook, stirring frequently, for 5 minutes. Stir in chili powder, oregano and cumin; season with salt and pepper to taste. Set aside.

Stir 3/4 cup (175 mL) of the Winter Salsa into refried beans; season with salt and pepper to taste. Spread 1/3 cup (75 mL) over each tortilla, leaving 1-inch (2.5 cm) border. Cover with vegetable mixture.

Roll up each tortilla and place, seam side down, in lightly greased 13- x 9-inch (3 L) baking dish. Bake in 400°F (200°C) oven for 15 minutes. Sprinkle with cheese; bake for 5 minutes longer or until heated through. Serve with yogurt and remaining salsa. Makes 5 servings.

	WINTER SALSA	
1	can (19 oz/540 mL) tomatoes	1
2 tsp	cider vinegar	10 mL
1-1/2 tsp	each ground cumin and chili powder	7 mL
4	green onions, chopped	4
1	clove garlic, minced	1
Half	sweet green pepper, chopped	Half
2 tbsp	chopped fresh coriander (optional)	25 mL

In food processor or by hand, chop tomatoes; transfer to bowl. Stir in vinegar, cumin, chili powder, onions, garlic, green pepper, and coriander (if using). (*Salsa can be refrigerated in airtight container for up to 2 days.*) Makes 3 cups (750 mL).

Buttermilk Pancakes

For a Mother's Day or Father's Day treat, why not mix up everyone's favorite breakfast food?
Older siblings can do the cooking and flipping while little ones set out maple syrup,
applesauce and yogurt for a choice of toppings.

1 cup	each all-purpose and whole wheat flours	250 mL
1 tbsp	granulated sugar	15 mL
1-1/2 tsp	baking powder	7 mL
1 tsp	baking soda	5 mL
2 cups	buttermilk	500 mL
2 tbsp	(approx) vegetable oil	25 mL
2	eggs, lightly beaten	2

In large bowl, combine all-purpose and whole wheat flours, sugar, baking powder and baking soda. Combine buttermilk, oil and eggs; stir into dry ingredients just until moistened. Let stand for 10 minutes.

꙳ Heat nonstick skillet over medium heat; brush lightly with oil. For each pancake, pour 1/4 cup (50 mL) batter into skillet, spreading slightly. Cook for 1-1/2 to 2 minutes or until underside is golden and bubbles break on top but don't fill in. Turn and cook for about 1 minute longer or until golden brown. Makes about 15 pancakes, enough for 4 servings.

THE BREAKFAST CLUB

If mornings are hectic at your house, the kids can learn to get their own breakfasts quite easily. Let them help you set the table and set out breakfast things the night before: boxes of cereal, fresh fruit, bread ready for the toaster, peanut butter. And check to make sure that there's juice made up and milk

for the cereal, preferably within reach of even young ones to help themselves in the morning. But if the thought of cereal leaves your child cold, try one of these:

꙳ *yogurt with fruit and toast*
꙳ *juice, yogurt and muffin*
꙳ *peanut butter on a bagel with sliced banana*

꙳ *egg salad or tuna salad sandwich and a glass of milk*
꙳ *bagel and cream cheese with a bunch of grapes*
꙳ *cheese and fruit*
꙳ *slice of leftover pizza (from last night's dinner) and a glass of milk*
꙳ *frozen banana pops (recipe, page 80)*

Pancake ABCs

*Shrove Tuesday, commonly known as Pancake Tuesday, is the perfect time for kids to
whip up a batch of delicious, fluffy pancakes for supper. For a fun twist, pour this smooth batter
into a squeeze bottle and create pancake letters and shapes.*

1-1/2 cups	all-purpose flour	375 mL
1 tbsp	baking powder	15 mL
1 tbsp	granulated sugar	15 mL
1/2 tsp	salt	2 mL
1-3/4 cups	milk	425 mL
2 tbsp	(approx) vegetable oil	25 mL
1	egg, lightly beaten	1

In large bowl, combine flour, baking powder, sugar and salt. Combine milk, oil and egg; stir into dry ingredients just until moistened. Pour into squeeze bottle.

🥄 Heat nonstick skillet over medium heat; brush lightly with oil. Squeeze batter, in batches, into skillet, creating different shapes. Cook for about 1 minute or until underside is golden and bubbles break on top but don't fill in. Turn and cook for about 30 seconds or until golden. Makes 24 small pancakes.

Chocolate Chip Cookies

*An all-time favorite, these cookies are crispy on the outside
and soft and chewy in the center. Little hands can help mix the dough, learn to
grease the pans and flatten the mounds before baking.*

1/2 cup	butter	125 mL
1/2 cup	shortening	125 mL
1 cup	granulated sugar	250 mL
1/2 cup	packed brown sugar	125 mL
2	eggs	2
2 tsp	vanilla	10 mL
2 cups	all-purpose flour	500 mL
1 tsp	baking soda	5 mL
1/2 tsp	salt	2 mL
2 cups	chocolate chips	500 mL
1 cup	chopped walnuts or pecans	250 mL

In large bowl, beat butter with shortening. Gradually beat in granulated and brown sugars. Beat in eggs and vanilla. Combine flour, baking soda and salt; blend into butter mixture. Stir in chocolate chips and nuts. Refrigerate for a few minutes or let stand at room temperature for 30 minutes.

Drop batter by tablespoonfuls (15 mL) onto lightly greased baking sheets. Flatten slightly to even 1/2-inch (1 cm) thickness. Bake in 375°F (190°C) oven for 8 to 9 minutes or until golden around edges. Let stand on baking sheet for 5 minutes. Transfer to racks; let cool completely. Makes about 48 cookies.

VARIATION

REVERSE CHOCOLATE CHIP COOKIES: Substitute 1/2 cup (125 mL) unsweetened cocoa powder for 1/2 cup (125 mL) of the all-purpose flour. Substitute white chocolate chips for regular chocolate chips.

Apple Cinnamon Muffins

*One of the easiest treats for kids to make is muffins. They mix up easily, cook quickly and
appeal to every age group. A fast, fun way to fill muffin pans is with an ice cream scoop.*

2 cups	all-purpose flour	500 mL
2/3 cup	granulated sugar	150 mL
1 tbsp	baking powder	15 mL
1/2 tsp	cinnamon	2 mL
3/4 cup	applesauce	175 mL
1/3 cup	butter, melted	75 mL
1	egg	1
1/2 cup	finely chopped peeled apple	125 mL
1/2 cup	raisins or chocolate chips (optional)	125 mL
	TOPPING	
2 tbsp	granulated sugar	25 mL
1/4 tsp	cinnamon	1 mL

In bowl, combine flour, sugar, baking powder and cinnamon. Whisk together applesauce, butter and egg; pour over dry ingredients. Add apple, and raisins (if using); stir just until dry ingredients are moistened. Spoon into greased muffin cups.

TOPPING: Mix sugar with cinnamon; sprinkle over batter. Bake in 375°F (190°C) oven for 25 minutes or just until tops are firm to the touch and cake tester inserted in centers comes out clean. Remove from pans and let cool on rack. Makes 12 muffins.

Banana Bran Carrot Mini Muffins

*These two-bite muffins are just the right size to tote to
school or to spread with cream cheese for a tasty after-school snack.*

1-1/2 cups	whole wheat flour	375 mL
1-1/2 cups	natural bran	375 mL
1 cup	grated carrot	250 mL
1/2 cup	wheat germ	125 mL
2 tsp	baking powder	10 mL
1 tsp	baking soda	5 mL
1/2 tsp	salt	2 mL
1 cup	milk	250 mL
1 cup	mashed ripe bananas	250 mL
1/2 cup	plain low-fat yogurt	125 mL
1/2 cup	vegetable oil	125 mL
1/4 cup	packed brown sugar	50 mL
1/4 cup	molasses	50 mL
2	eggs, beaten	2
1/2 cup	raisins	125 mL

In large bowl, combine flour, bran, carrot, wheat germ, baking powder, baking soda and salt.

Whisk together milk, bananas, yogurt, oil, sugar, molasses and eggs; pour over dry ingredients. Sprinkle with raisins; stir just until dry ingredients are moistened.

Spoon heaping tablespoonful (15 mL) batter into each well-greased 2-inch (5 cm) tart cup. Bake in 400°F (200°C) oven for 10 to 15 minutes or until tops spring back when lightly touched. Makes about 48 mini muffins.

Power Drink

For breakfast, lunch or a snack, this healthy milk shake is easy to make and even easier to enjoy.

Half	banana	Half
1/2 cup	2% milk	125 mL
1/2 cup	plain yogurt	125 mL
1/2 cup	sliced strawberries or blueberries	125 mL

In blender or food processor, purée together banana, milk, yogurt and strawberries. Makes four 1/2-cup (125 mL) servings.

Old-Fashioned Chocolate Shake

Get out the spoons for this thick chocolate treat. Adults and kids alike will adore it.

2 cups	vanilla ice cream	500 mL
1/2 cup	milk	125 mL
1/4 cup	Chocolate Syrup (recipe follows)	50 mL

In blender, blend ice cream, milk and Chocolate Syrup on low setting for 5 seconds. Pour into tall glasses and serve with spoons. Makes 2 servings.

CHOCOLATE SYRUP		
1/2 cup	unsweetened cocoa powder	125 mL
2 tbsp	granulated sugar	25 mL
1 cup	hot water	250 mL

🍫 In small saucepan, stir together cocoa and sugar; whisk in water until smooth. Bring to boil, stirring. Remove from heat and let cool. *(Syrup can be refrigerated in airtight container for up to 2 weeks.)* Makes 1 cup (250 mL).

Frozen Banana Pops

What child wouldn't eat breakfast when it appears in the form of a hand-held frozen treat?
Use any flavor of yogurt and, if you prefer, substitute chopped nuts or shredded coconut for the granola.

2	large bananas	2
1/2 cup	plain yogurt	125 mL
1/2 cup	granola	125 mL

Cut bananas into chunks about 4 inches (10 cm) long; insert wooden sticks for handles. Roll in yogurt, then granola. Freeze on foil-lined pan until firm; wrap in plastic wrap to store. Makes 4 servings.

Jelly Belly

Use any combination of fruit juices for this colorful kids' dessert.

2	pkg (each 7 g) unflavored gelatin	2
1-1/2 cups	raspberry-cranberry juice	375 mL
1-1/2 cups	grape juice	375 mL

In small saucepan, sprinkle 1 package of the gelatin over 1/4 cup (50 mL) water; let stand for 5 minutes or until softened.

🍇 Stir in 1/2 cup (125 mL) of the raspberry-cranberry juice; heat over low heat until gelatin dissolves. Remove from heat; stir in remaining raspberry-cranberry juice. Pour into 9- x 5-inch (1.5 L) loaf pan. Cover and refrigerate until firm, about 3 hours.

🍇 Repeat with remaining gelatin and grape juice; pour over firm raspberry-cranberry mixture. Refrigerate until firm, about 3 hours. To serve, slice and cut into cubes; spoon into bowls. Makes 6 servings.

TIP: A 2-cup (500 mL) bowl can be used instead of a loaf pan.

SIMPLE RECIPE IDEAS

🍃 **Instant Pudding**: Mix equal amounts of plain yogurt with applesauce or puréed banana.

🍃 **Dinosaur Toast**: Cut day-old bread slices into dinosaur shapes using cookie cutters, then toast in 350°F (180°C) oven for about 20 minutes or until golden brown.

🍃 **"Joosicles"**: Fill ice cube trays or Popsicle moulds with unsweetened fruit juice; place Popsicle sticks in center and freeze until firm. Keep a supply of "joosicles" in the freezer for snacks and for soothing sore throats.

🍃 **Make-your-own Meals**: For a special treat, let kids assemble their own tacos or pizzas. Put out small bowls of prepared ingredients — shredded lettuce, grated carrot, grated cheese, sliced cucumber, julienned chicken — along with taco shells or pita bread.

🍃 **Fancy low-fat Cakes**: Make up your child's favorite cake or muffin recipe in a cake pan. Once the cake has cooled, top it with a paper doily, sprinkle it with icing sugar, then remove the doily: presto, you've got a pretty snowflake pattern that turns a simple cake into something special without adding the extra fat, calories and sugar of icing or frosting.

Chapter Five

SPRING
at
LAST

Whisk away the winter blahs
with a veranda brunch,
a barbecue party, or a berry-
picking trip. It's spring!

(from left) Fruit Platter with Dip,
Celery Radish Slaw, Cheddar Quick Bread and
Mushroom and Spinach Crêpe Torte
(recipes, next page)

VERANDA BRUNCH
MENU

Cheddar Quick Bread*   Celery Radish Slaw*

Cinnamon Rolls   Fruit Platter with Dip*

Mushroom and Spinach Crêpe Torte*

Recipes included

Cheddar Quick Bread

This savory loaf is delicious with butter or a light spreading of whipped cream cheese.
Before guests arrive, reheat the loaf so its inviting fragrance greets them at the door.

2 cups	all-purpose flour	500 mL
2 cups	shredded old Cheddar cheese	500 mL
4 tsp	baking powder	20 mL
1 tbsp	granulated sugar	15 mL
3/4 tsp	dried oregano	4 mL
3/4 tsp	dry mustard	4 mL
1/2 tsp	salt	2 mL
1	egg	1
1 cup	milk	250 mL
1 tbsp	butter, melted	15 mL
6	green onions, finely chopped	6

In bowl, stir together flour, Cheddar cheese, baking powder, sugar, oregano, mustard and salt. Whisk together egg, milk and butter; add to dry ingredients along with onions, stirring until combined.

🍃 Spread in greased and floured 8-1/2- x 4-1/2-inch (1.5 L) loaf pan. Bake in 350°F (180°C) oven for 40 to 45 minutes or until tester inserted in center comes out clean. Let cool on rack for 10 minutes before turning out of pan. Serve warm. Makes 1 loaf.

Celery Radish Slaw

Radishes add color and crunch to this salad. Both the vegetables and
the dressing can be made the day before but refrigerated separately.

6 cups	thinly shredded savoy cabbage	1.5 L
3 cups	slivered radishes	750 mL
2 cups	thinly sliced celery	500 mL
1 cup	chopped green onions	250 mL
	DRESSING	
1/4 cup	lemon juice	50 mL
1 tsp	granulated sugar	5 mL
1 tsp	dry mustard	5 mL
3/4 tsp	salt	4 mL
1/4 tsp	pepper	1 mL
1/2 cup	vegetable oil	125 mL

In bowl, toss together cabbage, radishes, celery and onions.
🍃 DRESSING: In small bowl, combine lemon juice, sugar, mustard, salt and pepper; gradually whisk in oil. *(Salad and dressing can be covered and refrigerated separately for up to 1 day.)* Pour dressing over salad; toss well. Makes 8 servings.

Mushroom and Spinach Crêpe Torte

*For a special spring brunch, this make-ahead torte features crêpes layered with
cheesy sauced mushrooms and spinach. The torte can lay in wait in the refrigerator, ready and timed
to pop into the oven just before the first guests arrive.*

1 cup	all-purpose flour	250 mL
1/4 tsp	salt	1 mL
3	eggs	3
1-1/4 cups	milk	300 mL
3 tbsp	(approx) butter, melted	50 mL
	CHEESE SAUCE	
3 tbsp	butter	50 mL
3 tbsp	all-purpose flour	50 mL
2-1/2 cups	hot milk	625 mL
1/2 tsp	salt	2 mL
1/4 tsp	each pepper and ground nutmeg	1 mL
1/2 cup	whipping cream	125 mL
2 cups	shredded Swiss cheese	500 mL
	FILLING	
2 tbsp	butter	25 mL
1	onion, finely chopped	1
2	pkg (each 300 g) frozen chopped spinach, thawed and drained	2
5 cups	sliced mushrooms (about 1 lb/500 g)	1.25 mL
1/3 cup	freshly grated Parmesan cheese	75 mL

In bowl, combine flour and salt; make well in center. Whisk together eggs, milk and 2 tbsp (25 mL) of the butter; gradually pour into well, whisking to draw in flour until smooth. Cover and refrigerate for 1 hour; strain.

⁂ Heat 8-inch (20 cm) crêpe pan over medium heat until drop of water sprinkled on pan spatters briskly. Brush with some of the remaining butter. Pour in 2 tbsp (25 mL) batter for each crêpe, tilting pan to spread evenly; cook for 1 minute or until underside is starting to turn golden. Turn and cook for 30 to 60 seconds or until golden. (*Crêpes can be stacked between sheets of waxed paper, wrapped and refrigerated for up to 3 days or frozen for up to 2 months.*)

⁂ CHEESE SAUCE: In saucepan, melt butter over medium heat; cook flour, stirring, for 2 minutes, without browning. Gradually whisk in hot milk; add salt, pepper and nutmeg. Cook, whisking, for 5 to 7 minutes or until boiling and thickened. Stir in cream and 1-1/2 cups (375 mL) of the Swiss cheese until melted; set aside.

⁂ FILLING: In skillet, melt 1 tbsp (15 mL) of the butter over medium-low heat; cook half of the onion for 3 minutes or until softened. Add spinach; cook over medium-high heat, stirring, for about 5 minutes or until excess moisture has evaporated. Stir in 1-1/3 cups (325 mL) of the cheese sauce; transfer to bowl.

⁂ In clean skillet, melt remaining butter over medium-low heat; cook remaining onion for 3 minutes or until softened. Add mushrooms; cook over high heat, stirring often, for 5 to 7 minutes or until all moisture has evaporated. Stir in 1 cup (250 mL) of the cheese sauce and Parmesan cheese; set aside.

⁂ ASSEMBLY: Overlapping slightly, arrange 3 crêpes in single layer on bottom of 9-inch (2.5 L) springform pan; spread with 1 cup (250 mL) of the spinach filling. Top with 3 more crêpes; spread with half of the mushroom filling.

⁂ Repeat layering with 2 more additions of spinach and 1 of mushroom filling. Arrange 3 crêpes over top; spread with remaining cheese sauce. Sprinkle with remaining Swiss cheese. (*Torte can be prepared to this point, covered and refrigerated for up to 12 hours; remove from refrigerator 20 minutes before baking.*)

⁂ Bake in 350°F (180°C) oven for 50 to 60 minutes or until heated through and top is browned. Let stand in pan on rack for 30 minutes before serving in wedges. Makes 8 servings.

FRUIT PLATTER WITH DIP

Surround the dip with an assortment of fresh fruits: strawberries, raspberries, blackberries and cherries in early summer, sliced peaches, nectarines and melons later on. Provide fondue forks or toothpicks for smaller fruit. Garnish the platter with scented geranium petals and borage flowers.

⁂ DAIQUIRI DIP: Place 2 cups (500 mL) plain yogurt in cheesecloth-lined sieve set over bowl. Cover and refrigerate for 12 hours or until reduced to 1 cup (250 mL). Transfer to bowl; discard whey. Stir in 4 tsp (20 mL) granulated sugar, 4 tsp (20 mL) white rum, 1 tsp (5 mL) grated lime rind and 2 tsp (10 mL) lime juice. (Dip can be covered and refrigerated for up to 1 day; stir to blend.) Makes about 1 cup (250 mL).

TIP: You can substitute 1 cup (250 mL) sour cream for the drained yogurt, if desired, and fruit juice, such as pineapple or mango, for the rum.

Cinnamon Buns

Hot from the oven and fragrant, these cinnamon buns are gooey with caramel, nuts and lots of spice.

1/4 cup	granulated sugar	50 mL
1/2 cup	warm water	125 mL
1	pkg active dry yeast (or 1 tbsp/15 mL)	1
1/2 cup	milk	125 mL
1/4 cup	butter	50 mL
1 tsp	salt	5 mL
2	eggs, beaten	2
4 cups	(approx) all-purpose flour	1 L
	FILLING	
1 cup	butter	250 mL
1-1/2 cups	packed brown sugar	375 mL
1 cup	coarsely chopped pecans	250 mL
1 tbsp	cinnamon	15 mL

Dissolve 1 tsp (5 mL) of the sugar in warm water; sprinkle in yeast. Let stand for 10 minutes or until frothy. ❧ Meanwhile, in small saucepan, heat milk, remaining sugar, butter and salt until butter has melted; let cool to lukewarm.

❧ In large bowl, combine eggs, milk mixture and yeast mixture. Using electric mixer, gradually beat in 1-1/2 cups (375 mL) of the flour; beat for 2 minutes or until smooth.

With wooden spoon, gradually stir in enough of the remaining flour to make soft, slightly sticky dough. Turn out onto lightly floured surface; knead for 7 to 10 minutes or until smooth and elastic.

❧ Place dough in large greased bowl, turning to grease all over; cover with plastic wrap. Let rise in warm place for 1 to 1-1/2 hours (or in refrigerator for 8 hours) or until doubled in bulk and impression remains when fingertips are pressed into dough. Punch down dough.

❧ FILLING: Meanwhile, in saucepan over medium heat, melt 3/4 cup (175 mL) of the butter with 3/4 cup (175 mL) of the sugar, whisking until smooth. Pour into greased 13- x 9-inch (3 L) baking dish. Sprinkle with half of the pecans; set aside. Melt remaining butter; set aside. Combine remaining sugar, pecans and cinnamon; set aside.

❧ On lightly floured surface, roll out dough into 18- x 14-inch (45 x 35 cm) rectangle. Brush with all but 2 tbsp (25 mL) melted butter, leaving 1/2-inch (1 cm) border uncovered; sprinkle with sugar mixture.

❧ Starting at long side, tightly roll up, pinching seam to seal. Brush with remaining butter. With serrated knife, cut into 15 pieces; place, cut side down, in prepared pan. Cover and let rise for 1 hour or until doubled in bulk.

❧ Bake in 375°F (190°C) oven for 25 to 30 minutes or until golden and tops sound hollow when tapped. Let stand in pan for 3 minutes. Invert onto serving platter, scraping off any remaining filling in pan to drizzle over buns. Makes 15 buns.

Passover Sponge Cake

Feathery light, this sponge cake is the perfect finale to a meal. Garnish with orange slices and serve with fruit.

9	eggs, separated	9
1-1/4 cups	granulated sugar	300 mL
1 tbsp	finely grated orange rind	15 mL
1/3 cup	orange juice	75 mL
2/3 cup	potato starch	150 mL
1/3 cup	matzo cake meal	75 mL
1/3 cup	poppy seeds	75 mL

In large bowl, beat egg yolks with 1/2 cup (125 mL) of the sugar, orange rind and juice for about 10 minutes or until pale and thickened.

❧ In separate bowl and using clean beaters, beat egg whites until soft peaks form; gradually beat in remaining sugar until stiff peaks form.

❧ Sift together potato starch and matzo cake meal; stir in poppy seeds. Fold into egg yolk mixture alternately with egg whites, making 3 additions of each.

❧ Pour into ungreased 10-inch (4 L) tube pan. Bake in 325°F (160°C) oven for 50 to 60 minutes or until cake springs back when lightly touched. Turn pan upside down and let hang, on legs attached to pan or on inverted funnel, until completely cool. Makes 8 servings.

Quick Hot Cross Buns

Instant yeast helps you make hot cross buns in less than two hours.
Serve them fresh from the oven for an Easter brunch treat.

4 cups	(approx) all-purpose flour	1 L
1/4 cup	granulated sugar	50 mL
1	pkg quick-rising (instant) dry yeast (or 1 tbsp/15 mL)	1
1-3/4 tsp	cinnamon	9 mL
1 tsp	salt	5 mL
1 tsp	grated lemon rind	5 mL
1/2 tsp	each allspice and ground nutmeg	2 mL
1 cup	milk	250 mL
1/2 cup	water	125 mL
1/4 cup	butter	50 mL
2	eggs, lightly beaten	2
1/2 cup	mixed candied fruit	125 mL
1/2 cup	currants	125 mL
	GLAZE	
1	egg yolk	1
2 tbsp	milk	25 mL

	EASY ICING	
1 cup	icing sugar	250 mL
2 tbsp	(approx) milk	25 mL

In large bowl, stir together 3 cups (750 mL) of the flour, sugar, yeast, cinnamon, salt, lemon rind, allspice and ground nutmeg.

❧ In saucepan, heat milk, water and butter, stirring, until 125 to 130°F (50 to 55°C) on thermometer. Immediately add to flour mixture, stirring vigorously. Blend in eggs. With wooden spoon, stir in enough of the remaining flour to make soft, slightly sticky dough.

❧ On lightly floured surface, knead dough for 7 to 10 minutes or until smooth and elastic. Knead in candied fruit and currants. Cover with plastic wrap; let rest for 10 minutes.

❧ Divide dough into 12 portions; form into smooth balls. Place 2 inches (5 cm) apart on large greased baking sheet; flatten slightly. Cover with greased waxed paper; let rise in warm draft-free spot for about 45 minutes or until doubled in bulk. With serrated knife, slash shallow cross on top of each bun.

❧ GLAZE: Whisk egg yolk with milk; brush over buns. Bake in 375°F (190°C) oven for 20 to 25 minutes or until golden and bottoms sound hollow when tapped. Let cool on racks.

❧ EASY ICING: Stir icing sugar with enough of the milk to make liquid. Drizzle into crosses. Makes 12 buns.

Easter Eggs

The Anglican Church Women of All Saints Church in Peterborough, Ontario,
raise money for church projects by selling their delicious, chocolate-dipped, homemade Easter Eggs.
Here's an adaptation of their recipe which can be divided to make extra flavors.

1 cup	butter, softened	250 mL
3 lb	icing sugar	1.5 kg
2/3 cup	condensed milk	150 mL
1 tbsp	vanilla	15 mL
1/2 tsp	salt	2 mL
1 lb	semisweet chocolate, chopped	500 g
2 tbsp	vegetable shortening	25 mL
	ICING	
2 lb	icing sugar	1 kg
1 cup	vegetable shortening	250 mL
1/2 cup	milk	125 mL
	Food coloring (optional)	

In large bowl, beat butter until fluffy; gradually beat in icing sugar, condensed milk, vanilla and salt. Turn out onto work surface; knead until smooth. Shape into 32 eggs. Refrigerate for 1 hour or until firm.

❧ In bowl over hot (not boiling) water, melt chocolate with shortening; remove from heat. Using two forks, dip each egg into chocolate to coat; shake off excess. Place on waxed paper-lined baking sheets; refrigerate until chocolate is set.

❧ ICING: In large bowl, gradually beat sugar into shortening until fluffy. Beat in milk until smooth. Divide into batches; beat in food coloring (if using). Decorate eggs. Makes 32 eggs.

FLAVOR VARIATIONS (per one-quarter egg mixture):
❧ CHOCOLATE: Beat in 1 tbsp (15 mL) unsweetened cocoa powder.
❧ MAPLE WALNUT: Add 2 tbsp (25 mL) chopped walnuts and 1/2 tsp (2 mL) maple extract.
❧ CITRUS: Beat in 1 tbsp (15 mL) grated orange rind.

Saffron-Glazed Lamb

A special treat, lamb is a favorite whether you celebrate Easter or plan a Passover Seder supper.

1	boned rolled shoulder of lamb (2-1/2 lb/1.25 kg)	1
2	large cloves garlic, slivered	2
1 tsp	saffron threads	5 mL
3 tbsp	vegetable oil	50 mL
1/4 tsp	each salt and pepper	1 mL
1/4 cup	lemon juice	50 mL
2 cups	chicken stock	500 mL
2 tsp	flour or matzo meal	10 mL
	Salt and pepper	

Cut slits all over top of lamb; insert garlic slivers. In bowl, lightly crush 1/2 tsp (2 mL) of the saffron with back of spoon; stir in 1 tbsp (15 mL) of the oil, salt and pepper. Set roast, fat side up, on greased rack in shallow roasting pan; brush all over with saffron mixture. Let stand at room temperature for 30 minutes.

Meanwhile, in small bowl, whisk together remaining saffron, oil and lemon juice. Roast lamb in 450°F (230°C) oven for 15 minutes. Reduce heat to 325°F (160°C); pour half of the stock into pan. Roast, basting every 15 minutes with lemon mixture and turning halfway through cooking time, for 1 hour and 15 minutes or until meat thermometer registers 140°F (60°C) for rare. Transfer to warm platter; tent with foil.

Skim off any fat from pan juices. Over medium-high heat, stir in remaining stock, scraping up brown bits from pan. Sprinkle with flour or matzo meal; cook, whisking, for about 3 minutes or until boiling and thickened. Season with salt and pepper to taste. Serve with lamb. Makes 8 servings.

Fruit and Carrot Tsimmis

A colorful side dish of carrots, potatoes and dried fruits, tsimmes is a festive food usually included in a Passover Seder supper. It combines sweet and fruity and symbolizes good wishes for the year to come.

1/4 cup	margarine	50 mL
12	large carrots, sliced	12
6	potatoes, peeled and quartered	6
1	sweet potato, peeled and cut into 1-inch (2.5 cm) chunks	1
2 cups	chicken stock	500 mL
1-1/2 cups	orange juice	375 mL
1 cup	pitted prunes	250 mL
1/2 cup	raisins	125 mL
1/2 cup	dried apricots, quartered	125 mL
3 tbsp	liquid honey	50 mL
2 tsp	grated lemon rind	10 mL
1/4 cup	lemon juice	50 mL
2 tsp	cinnamon	10 mL
1 tsp	salt	5 mL
1/2 tsp	ground cloves	2 mL
1 tbsp	potato starch	15 mL
1/4 cup	cold water	50 mL

In large heavy saucepan, melt margarine over medium heat; stir in carrots, and white and sweet potatoes until coated. Pour in stock and orange juice; cover and bring to boil. Reduce heat to medium low; cook for 15 to 20 minutes or until vegetables are barely softened.

Add prunes, raisins, apricots, honey, lemon rind and juice, cinnamon, salt and cloves; cover and cook for about 20 minutes or until dried fruit has softened.

Blend potato starch into cold water; pour into vegetable mixture. Cook, stirring gently, for about 5 minutes or until thickened and vegetables are glazed. Makes 8 servings.

Spinach and Strawberry Salad

Strawberries are the most popular pick-your-own berries across the country.
This salad is a great way to serve spring's bounty.

1	pkg (10 oz/284 g) fresh spinach	1
2 cups	strawberries	500 mL
2	small oranges	2
1/3 cup	pecan halves, toasted	75 mL
	DRESSING	
1/3 cup	vegetable oil	75 mL
2 tbsp	strawberry or white wine vinegar	25 mL
1-1/2 tsp	granulated sugar	7 mL
1/4 tsp	salt	1 mL
Pinch	pepper	Pinch

Trim spinach; tear into pieces and place in salad bowl. Hull and halve strawberries; add to bowl. Peel oranges; with sharp knife, cut off thin outer membrane. Slice thinly crosswise, discarding any seeds; add to bowl. Chop pecans coarsely if desired; add to bowl.

❧ DRESSING: Whisk together oil, vinegar, sugar, salt and pepper; toss with salad. Makes 6 to 8 servings.

TIP: To toast pecans, bake on baking sheet in 350°F (180°C) oven for 5 to 10 minutes or until lightly golden; let cool.

PLANT A POT OF SPRINGTIME

Boost winter-weary spirits by coaxing bulbs into fragrant blooms — an affordable extravagance even on a slim budget.

YOU NEED:

🌿 Bowl, pot or jar (wide-based and watertight; clear glass shows growing roots)

🌿 Glass pebbles*, marbles, smooth river stones* or gravel (if using road gravel, wash off salt or oil)

🌿 Sheet moss* (optional)

🌿 Paperwhite or hyacinth bulbs*

* Available at nurseries and floral supply stores

TO MAKE:

1 Place 5 to 10 cm (2 to 4 inches) of glass pebbles in container. (Note: For clear container, you may wish to layer different materials.) Set bulbs on top — close together and right side up — stabilizing, if necessary, with a little extra material around each bulb until roots anchor bulbs in place. If desired, tuck moss between bulbs.

2 Add water until bulb tips are immersed just 3 mm (1/8 inch). Don't overfill or bulbs will rot.

3 For paperwhites: Place in sunny spot. Bulbs bloom in 4 to 6 weeks. For hyacinths: Place in shaded, cool spot. Bulbs will sprout in 8 to 12 weeks.

When sprouts are about 10 cm (4 inches) high, move bowl into semishade for a week, then move to sunny windowsill.

TIP: Bulbs bloom only once with this method, so start with fresh ones each time and keep correct water level constant.

Sesame Chicken with Asparagus

Fresh asparagus makes this quick and easy main dish perfect for a spring menu.
Serve it on a bed of rice or pasta.

1-1/2 lb	boneless skinless chicken breasts	750 g
1/4 cup	soy sauce	50 mL
2 tbsp	rice wine vinegar	25 mL
1 tbsp	sesame oil	15 mL
1 tbsp	liquid honey	15 mL
1/2 tsp	hot pepper sauce	2 mL
1 lb	asparagus, trimmed	500 g
2 tbsp	vegetable oil	25 mL
1	sweet red pepper, sliced	1
4	green onions, sliced	4
2 tsp	cornstarch	10 mL
2 tsp	sesame seeds, toasted	10 mL

Cut chicken into 3/4-inch (2 cm) wide strips.
In large bowl, combine soy sauce, vinegar, sesame oil, honey and hot pepper sauce; add chicken and marinate in refrigerator for at least 30 minutes or up to 8 hours. Drain, reserving marinade.

In shallow saucepan of boiling water, cook asparagus for 4 to 5 minutes or until tender-crisp; drain well and set aside.

In wok or skillet, heat vegetable oil over medium-high heat; stir-fry chicken, in batches, for 3 to 4 minutes or just until chicken is no longer pink inside. Remove and set aside.

Stir-fry red pepper for 1 minute; add to chicken. Stir-fry onions for 1 minute. Return chicken and red pepper to pan; add asparagus. Cook for 1 to 2 minutes or until heated through.

Combine cornstarch and reserved marinade; add to pan and cook, stirring, just until thickened and clear. Sprinkle with sesame seeds. Makes 4 to 6 servings.

Creamed Fiddleheads and Carrots

Use new carrots in this delightful side dish which goes beautifully with chicken or lamb.

3	carrots	3
2 tbsp	butter	25 mL
1 tbsp	finely chopped fresh chervil (or 1 tsp/5 mL dried)	15 mL
1 tsp	granulated sugar	5 mL
	Salt and pepper	
1/3 cup	water	75 mL
1/2 cup	whipping cream	125 mL
2 cups	fiddleheads	500 mL

Cut carrots into 2- x 1/2-inch (5 x 1 cm) strips. In large heavy skillet, melt butter over medium heat. Add carrots; sprinkle with chervil, sugar, and salt and pepper to taste. Cook, tossing to glaze, for 3 minutes.

Add water and reduce heat to medium-low; cover and simmer for 6 to 8 minutes or until almost tender. Increase heat to medium-high; uncover and cook until water evaporates. Add cream; cook for 2 to 4 minutes or until thickened.

Meanwhile, in saucepan of boiling water, cook fiddleheads for 5 to 7 minutes or until tender (for cleaning instructions, see next page). Drain well. Add to carrots. Makes 4 servings.

THE FIRST TASTES OF SPRING AND SUMMER

Harbingers of spring and summer, tender green vegetables such as fiddleheads, asparagus, spinach and fresh peas — sugar snap or regular garden variety — rate a special place in our meals. Just steamed to perfection, served with a flavored butter or cold in salads, there's nothing tastier.

❧ *FIDDLEHEADS: To clean fresh fiddleheads, uncurl each head; shake off the thin brown scaly husk. Wash fiddleheads several times in cool water; trim off dark stem ends. Two cups (500 mL) fresh fiddleheads makes 4 servings. Cook, uncovered, in a large amount of boiling salted water, or steam in basket set over boiling water, for 5 to 8 minutes or just until tender. Alternatively, microwave at High in*

small amount of water, covered, for 5 minutes; let stand, covered, for 3 minutes. Serve with butter and a squirt of lemon juice.

❧ *ASPARAGUS: Cook asparagus by laying spears in a wide saucepan of boiling salted water and gently boiling for 2 to 5 minutes or until tender-crisp. Or, cook in steamer basket over boiling water for the same time. To microwave: arrange 1 lb (500 g) fresh asparagus with tips to center of a large round pie plate. Add 2 tbsp (25 mL) water; cover and cook at High for 6 to 8 minutes, rotating once. Serve with butter, hollandaise or a light vinaigrette.*

❧ *SPINACH: Wash fresh spinach well; shake off excess water. With just the water clinging to leaves,*

cook spinach, covered, in large saucepan over medium-high heat only until wilted, about 5 minutes. Drain, squeezing out as much water as possible. Alternatively, microwave spinach at High, covered, for 4 to 5 minutes. Serve, buttered, with a sprinkle of toasted pine nuts.

❧ *GREEN PEAS: Sugar snap peas and snow peas are tender young vegetables, best when not overcooked. Add to stir-fries, steam or microwave them for best results. Cook 2 cups (500 mL) fresh shelled peas with a little water for 5 to 8 minutes or until just tender. Serve buttered, or with chopped fresh dill or mint. Nice with sautéed sliced green onions or mushrooms.*

Strawberry Rhubarb Pie

No one can resist this deep-pink winning combination. Easy to make, pretty to serve,
there's just a hint of spice in the filling.

	Pastry for 9-inch (23 cm) double-crust pie (see Perfect Pastry, page 138)	
4 cups	chopped rhubarb	1 L
2 cups	sliced strawberries	500 mL
1-1/3 cups	granulated sugar	325 mL
1/4 cup	cornstarch	50 mL
1 tbsp	lemon juice	15 mL
1/4 tsp	cinnamon	1 mL
1	egg, beaten	1

On lightly floured surface, roll out half of the pastry; fit into 9-inch (23 cm) pie plate. Set aside.
⟐ In bowl, combine rhubarb, strawberries, sugar, cornstarch, lemon juice and cinnamon; spoon into pie shells. Brush pastry rim with some of the egg.
⟐ Roll out remaining pastry; using pastry wheel or knife, cut into 1-inch (2.5 cm) wide strips. Gently weave strips over pie to form lattice; trim and flute edge. Brush lattice with egg.
⟐ Bake on baking sheet in 425°F (220°C) oven for 15 minutes. Reduce heat to 375°F (190°C); bake for 50 to 60 minutes longer or until rhubarb is tender, filling thickened and crust golden. Makes 8 servings.

Rhubarb Compote with Strawberries

A combination of icy-cold stewed rhubarb and freshly sliced strawberries is sensational. Serve with
whipped cream and a dash of cinnamon, or plain or strawberry-flavored yogurt.

1/2 cup	packed brown sugar	125 mL
1/4 cup	orange juice	50 mL
4 cups	chopped fresh rhubarb	1 L
2 cups	sliced fresh strawberries	500 mL
	Whipped cream or yogurt	
	Cinnamon	

In large saucepan, bring sugar and orange juice to boil over medium heat; add rhubarb. Cover and reduce heat to low; simmer, stirring occasionally, for 5 to 8 minutes or until rhubarb is tender. Let cool; refrigerate until chilled or for up to 2 days.
⟐ To serve, stir in strawberries; spoon into stemmed glasses. Dollop with whipped cream and sprinkle with cinnamon to taste. Makes 4 servings.

Quebec Maple Syrup Pie

In Quebec, Easter coincides with the maple syrup season and Easter dinner
often features this classic sweet "Tarte au Sirop d'Erable".

	Pastry for 9-inch (23 cm) single-crust pie (see Perfect Pastry, page 138)	
2-1/4 cups	maple syrup	550 mL
3/4 cup	light cream	175 mL
1/4 cup	all-purpose flour	50 mL
4	eggs	4
1 cup	walnuts (optional)	250 mL

On lightly floured surface, roll out pastry to 1/8-inch (3 mm) thickness; fit into 9-inch (23 cm) pie plate. Trim and crimp edges. With fork, prick crust all over; chill in freezer for 30 minutes.
⟐ In bowl, whisk together maple syrup, cream, flour and eggs until blended; stir in nuts (if using). Pour into crust. Bake in 375°F (190°C) oven for 10 minutes; reduce heat to 350°F (180°C) and bake for 30 to 35 minutes longer or until set. Let cool on rack. Makes 8 servings.

Strawberry Rhubarb Pie

Rhubarb Kuchen

A wonderful blend of tart, tangy rhubarb and a thick, buttery almond crust, this dessert is best served the same day it's made. Enjoy it fresh from the oven for brunch, afternoon tea or as a fine finale to Sunday dinner.

3/4 cup	butter, softened	175 mL
1-1/4 cups	granulated sugar	300 mL
1/3 cup	plain yogurt	75 mL
1	egg yolk	1
1 tsp	grated orange rind	5 mL
2 cups	all-purpose flour	500 mL

1/2 tsp	baking soda	2 mL
Pinch	salt	Pinch
3/4 cup	sliced almonds	175 mL
5 cups	chopped rhubarb (1-inch/2.5 cm pieces)	1.25 L
1 tbsp	orange juice	15 mL
	GLAZE	
1/3 cup	strawberry jelly	75 mL

In bowl, beat butter with 3/4 cup (175 mL) of the sugar; beat in yogurt, egg yolk and orange rind.

Combine flour, baking soda and salt; stir in 1/2 cup (125 mL) of the almonds. Gradually stir into butter mixture until combined. Using wet spatula or hands, spread dough evenly onto bottom and 3/4 inch (2 cm) up side of greased 10-inch (3 L) springform pan.

Toss rhubarb with remaining sugar and orange juice; arrange evenly over dough. Sprinkle remaining almonds around edge. Bake in 350°F (180°C) oven for 45 to 50 minutes or until pastry edge is golden brown and rhubarb is tender. Let cool on rack. Remove side of pan.

GLAZE: In small saucepan, bring strawberry jelly and 3 tbsp (50 mL) water to boil, whisking constantly. Reduce heat and simmer, whisking often, for about 3 minutes or until thickened. Brush over rhubarb and sides of cake. Let stand for 5 minutes. Makes 12 servings.

TIPS FOR PICK-YOUR-OWN TRIPS

There's a romance to indulging in the harvest of dewy-fresh vegetables from the field and berries straight from the patch. U-pick farms along the back roads of most provinces offer a chance to be make-believe farmers without all the hard work. And somehow the berries taste sweeter, the boxes or pails fill quickly and you can almost get home with the dew still on the fruit. And the price is right. Here are tips to help you get the best results in the field and get your produce home as fresh as possible.

✌ *Phone ahead.* Mother nature and crowds of visitors can mean slim pickings or no pickings at all.

✌ *Check to see if children are welcome.* At the same time, you may want to know about play areas and picnic tables.

✌ *Beat the heat:* pick in the cool of early morning or late afternoon.

✌ *Cool comfortable clothes,* a sun hat, boots for wet fields, sun block and insect repellent are handy items to make picking a pleasure.

✌ *Take along suitable containers.* Remember, smaller containers are best for berries. Large ones mean that bottom layers may arrive home crushed.

✌ *Coolers with ice packs* are a good thing to have in the car to get "field heat" out of berries and veggies as soon as possible.

SPRING BARBECUE PARTY
MENU FOR 20

Curried Shrimp Kabobs*

Assorted Breads

Rosemary Lemon Barbecued Chicken*

Corn with Parmesan Herb Butter*

Potato Salad

Two-Bean Salad with Garlic Vinaigrette*

Fresh Fruit Basket

Recipes included

Rosemary Lemon Barbecued Chicken

Rosemary, the herb of remembrance, adds a fragrant flavor to chicken that's truly memorable.

9 lb	chicken pieces	4 kg
	MARINADE	
4	cloves garlic, minced	4
1/3 cup	grated lemon rind	75 mL
1 cup	lemon juice	250 mL
1/3 cup	olive oil	75 mL
3 tbsp	chopped fresh rosemary (or 1 tbsp/15 mL dried)	50 mL
1/4 tsp	pepper	1 mL

Arrange chicken in two large baking dishes.
🍃 MARINADE: Whisk together garlic, lemon rind and juice, oil, rosemary and pepper; pour over chicken. Cover and refrigerate for at least 2 hours or up to 12 hours, turning occasionally.
🍃 Reserving marinade, place chicken on greased grill over medium heat; cook for 15 minutes. Turn and baste with marinade; cook for 10 to 15 minutes longer or until skin is crisp and juices run clear when chicken is pierced with fork. Makes 20 servings.

TIPS: 🍃 **Buy three broiler chickens and cut them up into eight pieces each, or purchase two dozen chicken pieces already cut up.**
🍃 **Microwave/Barbecue Cooking Method: Reserving marinade, place 8 chicken pieces at a time on microwave roasting rack with meatier portions toward outside; cover with waxed paper and microwave at High, turning pieces over once, for 8 to 10 minutes or until juices run clear when chicken is pierced. Place on greased grill over medium heat; cook for 10 minutes, turning and basting once with marinade. Makes 20 servings.**

Curried Shrimp Kabobs

Team these curry-marinated shrimp with pineapple for a popular appetizer.

1-1/3 lb	medium shrimp, peeled and deveined (about 40)	675 g
1	can (19 oz/540 mL) unsweetened pineapple chunks, drained	1
	MARINADE	
1/4 cup	lemon juice	50 mL
1/4 cup	olive oil	50 mL
1 tbsp	curry powder	15 mL
1 tsp	ground ginger	5 mL
1 tsp	chopped fresh mint	5 mL
2	cloves garlic, minced	2

MARINADE: In large bowl, whisk together lemon juice, oil, curry powder, ginger, mint and garlic; add shrimp, tossing to coat. Cover and refrigerate for at least 2 hours or up to 12 hours, stirring occasionally.

❧ Reserving marinade, thread 2 shrimp and pineapple wedges onto each soaked wooden skewer. Place on greased grill over medium heat; cook, basting with marinade and turning often, for about 5 minutes or until shrimp are pink. Makes 20 appetizers.

TIP: The shrimp can be peeled and deveined the day before, then marinated the day of the party. Be careful not to overcook shrimp or they'll be tough and dry.

Corn with Parmesan Herb Butter

Enjoy fresh corn steamed, boiled or grilled, then served with flavored butter, which can be prepared in advance and frozen for up to one month.

24	corn cobs (unhusked)	24
	PARMESAN HERB BUTTER	
1 cup	butter, softened	250 mL
1/4 cup	finely chopped fresh basil or parsley	50 mL
1/4 cup	freshly grated Parmesan cheese	50 mL
1/4 tsp	pepper	1 mL

PARMESAN HERB BUTTER: In bowl, blend together butter, basil, Parmesan and pepper. Divide between 2 sheets of waxed paper; shape into 1-inch (2.5 cm) diameter log, wrapping well. Freeze for about 2 hours or until firm. Let stand at room temperature for up to 20 minutes before slicing.

❧ Steamed: Husk corn and place on rack or in steamer over 2 inches (5 cm) of boiling water; cover and steam for 3 to 7 minutes or until tender.

❧ Boiled: Husk corn; cook in large pot of boiling water, covered, for 3 to 7 minutes or until tender.

❧ Grilled: Peel back husks and remove silk; rewrap husks and tie with string. Soak corn in cold water for 15 minutes. Place on grill over high heat; cook, turning frequently, for about 15 minutes or until tender. Makes 24 corn cobs and 1-1/4 cups (300 mL) butter.

Two-Bean Salad with Garlic Vinaigrette

A pleasant change from a sweet bean salad, this zesty version can be made using all green beans, if you prefer.

2 lb	green beans	1 kg
2 lb	yellow wax beans	1 kg
	Salt and pepper	
	GARLIC VINAIGRETTE	
1/3 cup	red wine vinegar	75 mL
1 tbsp	grainy mustard	15 mL
1 tsp	liquid honey	5 mL
3	cloves garlic, minced	3
1/2 cup	extra virgin olive oil	125 mL
1/2 cup	vegetable oil	125 mL

In large pot of boiling salted water, cook green and yellow beans for 3 to 5 minutes or until tender-crisp. Drain and refresh under cold water; drain again and pat dry. *(Beans can be wrapped in tea towel and refrigerated for up to 1 day.)*

🍃 GARLIC VINAIGRETTE: In bowl, whisk together vinegar, mustard, honey and garlic; gradually whisk in olive and vegetable oils.

🍃 Just before serving, toss beans with vinaigrette. Season with salt and pepper to taste. Makes 20 servings.

Spinach and Beef Salad

This unusual steak-and-salad supper packs a lot of nutrients into a low-calorie meal that's delicious enough to serve to guests.

1-1/2 cups	small pasta shells	375 mL
1/2 lb	sirloin steak, 1/2 inch (1 cm) thick	250 g
8 cups	torn spinach leaves	2 L
2 cups	watercress leaves	500 mL
4	green onions, thinly sliced	4
1 cup	sliced strawberries	250 mL
1 cup	thinly sliced radishes	250 mL
2 tbsp	chopped fresh mint	25 mL
1/3 cup	frozen orange juice concentrate, thawed	75 mL
2 tbsp	olive oil	25 mL
1/2 tsp	Dijon mustard	2 mL
	Pepper	

In saucepan of boiling salted water, cook pasta for 8 to 10 minutes or until tender but firm. Drain and rinse under cold water; drain again.

🍃 Meanwhile, cook steak on greased grill over high heat for 3 to 4 minutes per side for medium,

or to desired doneness. Let cool slightly. Trim off fat; slice thinly and place in salad bowl.

🍃 Add pasta, spinach, watercress, onions, strawberries, radishes and mint.

🍃 Whisk together orange juice concentrate, oil and mustard; toss with salad. Season with pepper to taste. Makes 4 servings.

Chapter Six

HURRAY *for* SUMMER

Summer's glorious weather spells picnics, barbecues and family reunions. Salads, burgers and berries feature in our cool cooking.

Terrific Burgers

Here's a juicy burger, perfect for all your favorite fixings.

1	egg	1
1/4 cup	dry bread crumbs	50 mL
1	small onion, grated	1
1	clove garlic, minced	1
1-1/2 tsp	dry mustard	7 mL
1/2 tsp	salt	2 mL
1/4 tsp	pepper	1 mL
1/4 tsp	Worcestershire sauce	1 mL
1 lb	lean ground beef	500 g
6	hamburger buns	6

In bowl, beat egg; mix in 2 tbsp (25 mL) water, bread crumbs, onion, garlic, mustard, salt, pepper and Worcestershire sauce. Mix in beef; shape into six 3/4-inch (2 cm) thick patties.
❧ Place on greased grill over medium-high heat; cook for 6 minutes per side or until no longer pink inside. Sandwich in buns. Makes 6 servings.

Barbecued Sesame Short Ribs

Don't pass over beef short ribs for the barbecue. These ribs are especially flavorful basted with sesame-ginger sauce.

3 lb	beef short ribs	1.5 kg
1 cup	water	250 mL
1/2 cup	soy sauce	125 mL
1/4 cup	packed brown sugar	50 mL
2 tbsp	minced gingerroot (or 1 tsp/5 mL ground ginger)	25 mL
1	clove garlic, minced	1
2 tbsp	liquid honey	25 mL
1 tbsp	sesame oil	15 mL
2 tbsp	sesame seeds, toasted	25 mL

In large saucepan, combine ribs, water, soy sauce, sugar, ginger and garlic; bring to boil. Reduce heat, cover and simmer, turning ribs occasionally, for about 1 hour or until ribs are tender. With slotted spoon, remove ribs and set aside.

➤ To saucepan, add honey and sesame oil; bring to boil and cook for 10 to 15 minutes or until sauce is reduced to 1 cup (250 mL).

➤ Place ribs on greased grill over medium heat; cook, turning and basting occasionally with sauce, for 10 to 15 minutes or until glazed and browned. Transfer to serving platter; sprinkle with sesame seeds. Makes 4 servings.

TIP: Beef short ribs should always be precooked before grilling to tenderize the meat and reduce the fat.

BURGER TIPS AND TOPPINGS

TIPS FOR BEST BURGERS

➤ *Lean and medium ground beef are both suitable for burgers. Although lean is lower in fat, fat does drip off medium ground beef during grilling — and medium is often on sale, especially during barbecue season.*

➤ *To be safe, always cook burgers until no longer pink inside.*

➤ *Add liquid, such as water or milk, to the ground meat mixture to ensure a juicy burger.*

➤ *When forming patties, press ingredients together lightly. If mixture is too compact, the cooked meat will be tough.*

➤ *Buttered buns? No way. Toast them, then try some of the specialty mustards such as Dijon or Russian-style. Or spread buns with light mayonnaise, herbed cream cheese*

or trendy tapenade, guacamole or pesto.

➤ *And why not try something other than plain hamburger buns? For a change, there's whole wheat buns, kaiser rolls, Portuguese pada buns or pita breads. Round foccacia, sliced horizontally, or thick baguettes cut into wide slices and hinged open, work well.*

TOPPINGS

➤ *A freshly made salsa livens up burgers, but they're also delicious with the store-bought variety. For a Tomato Rosemary Salsa: Gently stir together 1 large tomato, seeded and diced, 3 tbsp (50 mL) finely chopped green onions, 1 tbsp (15 mL) olive oil, 2 tsp (10 mL) chopped fresh rosemary, 2 tsp (10 mL) red wine vinegar, and 1/4 tsp (1 mL) each salt and pepper.*

Let stand at room temperature for 30 minutes to allow flavors to blend. Makes 2/3 cup (150 mL).

➤ *Serve a quick Garlic Sauce: Stir together 1/2 cup (125 mL) light sour cream, 1 tbsp (15 mL) light mayonnaise and 1 clove garlic, minced.*

➤ *Top burgers with sauerkraut and sliced dill pickles; serve sandwich-style on toasted dark rye bread.*

➤ *Bring out your favorite pickles and relishes. Trade in the usual mustard and relish for corn or zucchini relish, bread-and-butter pickles, pickled sliced sweet and hot peppers, chutney or Oriental sauces.*

Spiced Flank Steak

A spice rub gives flank steak a lot of flavor and adds a pleasant heat.

4 tsp	chili powder	20 mL
1-1/2 tsp	each dried thyme, oregano and coriander	7 mL
1-1/2 tsp	ground cumin	7 mL
1 tsp	pepper	5 mL
1/2 tsp	salt	2 mL
1	flank steak (about 2 lb/1 kg)	1

Combine chili powder, thyme, oregano, coriander, cumin, pepper and salt; rub over steak. Let stand at room temperature for 30 minutes or cover and refrigerate for up to 8 hours. Remove from refrigerator 30 minutes before grilling.

᪐ Place steak on greased grill over medium-high heat; cover and cook for 5 minutes per side for medium-rare or until desired doneness. Transfer to platter; tent with foil and let stand for 5 minutes. Slice thinly across the grain. Makes 8 servings.

TIP: There's a trick to cutting and carving less tender meats. Always cut across the grain into thin slices. This way, you're cutting through the tissues, and that makes the meat seem more tender.

Micro-Barbecued Spareribs

Team your microwave with your barbecue for winning results. Ribs stay moist, tender and juicy inside (thanks to microwave precooking) yet crispy and golden outside (courtesy of the barbecue).

3 lb	pork back ribs	1.5 kg
1/4 cup	water	50 mL
	BARBECUE SAUCE	
1/2 cup	ketchup	125 mL
2 tbsp	soy sauce	25 mL
1 tbsp	packed brown sugar	15 mL
1 tsp	minced gingerroot	5 mL
1 tsp	sesame oil	5 mL
1	clove garlic, minced	1

Cut ribs into serving-size pieces; place in 12-cup (3 L) microwaveable casserole. Add water; cover and microwave at High for 5 minutes. Microwave at Medium (50%) for 30 to 40 minutes or until meat is tender and no longer pink inside, rearranging twice. Drain well.

᪐ BARBECUE SAUCE: Combine ketchup, soy sauce, sugar, ginger, sesame oil and garlic.

᪐ Place ribs on greased grill over medium-high heat; brush with sauce. Cook, turning and basting with sauce once, for 10 minutes or until crisp and glazed. Makes 4 servings.

Grilled Salmon

Salmon, Atlantic or Pacific, is a favorite for barbecue fans from coast to coast. Choose a thick,
even fillet and let it soak up the Oriental flavors of this marinade before grilling slowly over a low heat.

2 lb	salmon fillet (unskinned)	1 kg
2 tbsp	each vegetable oil, lemon juice and soy sauce	25 mL
1 tbsp	each packed brown sugar and minced gingerroot	15 mL
2	cloves garlic, minced	2
Pinch	each pepper and cayenne pepper	Pinch

Make several shallow diagonal slashes in skinless side of salmon. Place, skin side up, in shallow glass dish. Whisk together oil, lemon juice, soy sauce, sugar, ginger, garlic, pepper and cayenne; pour over salmon and let stand for 30 minutes.

Discarding marinade, place fillet, skin side down, on greased grill over low heat; cover and cook for about 30 minutes or until fish flakes easily when tested with fork. Makes 6 servings.

Saucy Chicken Legs

Barbecued chicken — smoky, juicy, crisp — is specially tasty when brushed with a tangy barbecue sauce during cooking. Use half of this sauce for the chicken legs and refrigerate the rest to use on ribs or burgers.

6	chicken legs (about 3-1/2 lb/1.6 kg)	6
	BARBECUE SAUCE	
2 tbsp	vegetable oil	25 mL
1	onion, finely chopped	1
2	cloves garlic, minced	2
3/4 cup	chili sauce	175 mL
1/2 cup	cider vinegar	125 mL
1/4 cup	ketchup	50 mL
1/4 cup	orange juice	50 mL
2 tbsp	packed brown sugar	25 mL
2 tbsp	prepared horseradish	25 mL
1 tbsp	prepared mustard	15 mL
1 tbsp	Worcestershire sauce	15 mL
1/2 tsp	each dried oregano and thyme	2 mL

BARBECUE SAUCE: In saucepan, heat oil over medium-low heat; cook onion and garlic, stirring occasionally, for about 7 minutes or until very soft.

🍂 Stir in chili sauce, vinegar, ketchup, orange juice, sugar, horseradish, mustard, Worcestershire sauce, oregano and thyme; bring to boil. Reduce heat and simmer, stirring occasionally, for 20 minutes. Let cool. Cover and refrigerate half of the sauce for another use. (*Sauce can be covered and refrigerated for up to 2 weeks.*)

🍂 Place chicken legs on greased grill over medium-high heat; cook, meaty side up, for 20 minutes. Turn chicken; cook, turning and basting with sauce every 5 minutes, for 10 to 20 minutes or until juices run clear when chicken is pierced. Makes 6 servings.

SAUCES, RUBS AND MARINADES

A basting sauce can be as simple as a herb-flavored oil or melted butter, or a cooked sauce such as the tomato-based Barbecue Sauce (above). Basters with high sugar content or tomato should only be used in the last few minutes of cooking, to prevent charring.

A marinade contains an acidic ingredient — lemon juice, vinegar, wine or yogurt — to tenderize the meat, as well as herbs, spices or vegetables to add flavor.

🍂 *ORIENTAL MARINADE:* Combine 1/4 cup (50 mL) soy sauce, 2 tbsp (25 mL) rice vinegar, 2 tbsp (25 mL) vegetable oil, 1 tbsp (15 mL) minced gingerroot, 1 tbsp (15 mL) sesame oil, 2 cloves garlic, minced, and 1/4 tsp (1 mL) pepper. Makes enough for 1 lb (500 g) round steak or 2 lb (1 kg) chicken pieces.

🍂 *WINE VINEGAR MARINADE:* Combine 1/3 cup (75 mL) red wine vinegar, 3 tbsp (50 mL) vegetable oil, 2 tbsp (25 mL) chopped fresh basil, 1 tbsp (15 mL) Dijon mustard, 2 cloves garlic, minced, and 1/4 tsp (1 mL) pepper. Makes enough for 1 lb (500 g) round or flank steak.

A dry rub is a mixture of seasonings, usually spices or herbs, often mixed with just enough oil to make them cling to food.

🍂 *SPICY RUB FOR BEEF:* Combine 4 tsp (20 mL) chili powder, 1-1/2 tsp (7 mL) each dried thyme, oregano, cumin and coriander, 1 tsp (5 mL) pepper and 1/2 tsp (2 mL) salt. Rub over meat; let stand at room temperature for 30 minutes or marinate in refrigerator for up to 8 hours. Remove meat from refrigerator 30 minutes before grilling. Makes enough for 2 lb (1 kg) flank steak.

FAMILY REUNION BARBECUE

M E N U

Bean and Roasted Red Pepper Salad*	Cucumber Salad with Lime Dressing (p. 117)
Golden Oven-Fried Chicken*	Strawberry Shortcake (p. 129)
Pasta Salad	

Recipes included

Bean and Roasted Red Pepper Salad

Here's a new twist to an old favorite make-ahead salad. You can buy roasted sweet peppers in a jar if you don't want to roast your own.

2	cans (each 19 oz/540 mL) romano beans	2
1/4 cup	olive oil	50 mL
2 tbsp	red wine vinegar	25 mL
1 tbsp	finely chopped hot pepper	15 mL
1 tbsp	chopped fresh parsley	15 mL
1/2 tsp	each granulated sugar, dried basil and salt	2 mL
1/4 tsp	pepper	1 mL
1	clove garlic, minced	1
4	green onions, sliced	4
1/2 cup	chopped roasted sweet red pepper (see page 119)	125 mL
2	stalks celery, sliced	2

In saucepan, heat romano beans over medium-low heat until hot; drain and rinse under hot water. Drain well and place in bowl.

❧ Meanwhile, whisk together oil, vinegar, hot pepper, parsley, sugar, basil, salt, pepper and garlic; toss with beans. Stir in onions, roasted peppers and celery. Cover and refrigerate for at least 2 hours or until chilled. *(Salad can be stored in refrigerator for up to 1 week.)* Makes 10 servings.

Golden Oven-Fried Chicken

A summer gathering is a perfect occasion to offer a big batch of fried chicken. This oven method is easy to make and delicious to serve hot at home or cold at a picnic.

1 tbsp	each butter and vegetable oil	15 mL
1-1/2 cups	dry bread crumbs	375 mL
1 tbsp	paprika	15 mL
1-1/2 tsp	each dried marjoram, dry mustard and pepper	7 mL
3/4 tsp	salt	4 mL
2	cloves garlic, minced	2
2/3 cup	milk	150 mL
10	chicken legs, separated (3 lb/1.5 kg)	10

In rimmed baking sheet, melt butter with oil in 375°F (190°C) oven, tilting pan to coat evenly.

❧ In dish, combine bread crumbs, paprika, marjoram, mustard, pepper, salt and garlic. Pour milk into another dish. Dip chicken into crumb mixture, then into milk and again into crumb mixture to coat well.

❧ Arrange chicken, meaty side down, on prepared baking sheet; bake for 20 minutes.

❧ Turn chicken over; bake for 20 to 25 minutes or until juices run clear when chicken is pierced. Makes 10 servings.

FAMILY REUNIONS

*Summertime is family reunion time and potluck
suppers fill the bill nicely. If you can't get the family
together, you can always invite the neighbors or
surrounding cottagers for a party.
Here are a few tips:*

❧

*Be sure to plan well in advance,
and delegate jobs.*

❧

*You may want everyone to share expenses,
so that no family spends more than another.*

❧

*Unless a relative or family is noted
for a special dish that will fit into your menu easily,
assign appetizers, salads and desserts.*

❧

*Often the host family can handle the main course,
especially if it's to be barbecued.*

❧

*Get all generations involved.
Sharing skills with the young can be fun.*

❧

*Plan activities: sports events for the
active group, slide shows and photo album showings
for those less active.*

❧

*Follow up with a lasting memento.
Ask each contributor for a recipe, then send out
copies of the collection.*

❧

Take it easy. Relax and enjoy the reunion.

Pan Bagnat

This hearty Provençal sandwich bursts with the flavors of summer.
Perfect picnic fare, pan bagnat (literally "bathed bread") probably had its origins in
salade niçoise. Look for the smallest capers, marked "nonpareil."

1	large flat round Italian bread	1
3	large tomatoes, sliced	3
1	onion, thinly sliced	1
1	large sweet yellow pepper, cut into thin strips	1
1	can (7 oz/198 g) white tuna, drained	1
1	can (2 oz/50 g) anchovies, drained	1
1 cup	black olives (Kalamata or sun-dried), pitted	250 mL
1 cup	loosely packed fresh basil	250 mL
2 tbsp	capers, drained and rinsed	25 mL

	DRESSING	
3 tbsp	red wine vinegar	50 mL
1 tbsp	Dijon mustard	15 mL
2	cloves garlic, minced	2
1/4 tsp	pepper	1 mL
1/3 cup	olive oil	75 mL

Cut bread in half horizontally; hollow out bottom half, leaving 1-inch (2.5 cm) thick walls. Reserve crumbs for another use.

🍂 Layer tomatoes, onion and yellow pepper over base. Crumble tuna evenly over top. Using scissors, snip anchovies into small pieces; sprinkle over tuna. Scatter olives, basil and capers over top.

🍂 DRESSING: In small bowl, mix vinegar, mustard, garlic and pepper; gradually whisk in oil. Pour over filling.

🍂 Replace top of loaf; wrap tightly in foil. Weigh down with heavy weight; refrigerate for 2 hours or up to 4 hours. Cut into wedges to serve. Makes 8 servings.

Potato Salad with Pesto Mayonnaise

Mellow Mediterranean flavors blend in this hearty salad, best served at room temperature.

6	new potatoes (2 lb/1 kg)	6
1/3 cup	mayonnaise	75 mL
1/4 cup	Pesto (recipe follows)	50 mL
1/2 cup	pitted black olives	125 mL
	Salt and pepper	

	PESTO	
3	cloves garlic	3
1/3 cup	pine nuts, toasted	75 mL
2 cups	packed fresh basil leaves	500 mL
1/3 cup	freshly grated Parmesan cheese	75 mL
1/3 cup	olive oil	75 mL
	Salt and pepper	

Cut potatoes into 1-inch (2.5 cm) chunks. In saucepan of boiling salted water, cook potatoes for 12 to 14 minutes or just until tender. Drain and let cool.

🍂 In large bowl, combine mayonnaise with Pesto. Add potatoes and olives; toss to coat. Season with salt and pepper to taste. *(Salad can be covered and refrigerated for up to 4 hours; bring to room temperature before serving.)* Makes 6 servings.

🍂 In food processor or blender, mince garlic and pine nuts. Add basil, Parmesan cheese and oil; blend until smooth. Season with salt and pepper to taste. Makes 3/4 cup (175 mL). See Pesto Perks, opposite page, for leftover tips.

PESTO PERKS

If you think pesto is only for pasta, try these for zing.

❧ *Cut a baguette into 1/2-inch (1 cm) thick slices; spread with pesto and sprinkle with chopped sun-dried tomatoes and shredded mozzarella. Broil just until cheese melts. Serve hot as an appetizer (photo, below).*

❧ *Stir a spoonful into a bowl of homemade vegetable soup.*

❧ *Mix 2 tbsp (25 mL) pesto with 1 tbsp (15 mL) vegetable oil and 2 tsp (10 mL) white wine vinegar for a pesto vinaigrette to top sliced tomatoes.*

❧ *Mix equal quantities of pesto and soft butter. On plastic wrap, shape into 1-inch (2.5 cm) diameter log; wrap and freeze. Use slices to flavor hot vegetables, baked potatoes and barbecued meat or seafood.*

❧ *Brush fish, shrimp or chicken breasts with pesto before baking.*

❧ *Place chicken breast between plastic wrap and pound to 1/4-inch (5 mm) thickness. Combine 1 tbsp (15 mL) pesto with 1 tbsp (15 mL) ricotta cheese. Spoon onto center of breast; fold ends over and roll up. Bake in 350°F (180°C) oven for 40 to 45 minutes or until chicken is no longer pink inside.*

❧ *Roll out prepared bread dough into rectangle 1/4 inch (5 mm) thick; spread with pesto and roll up, jelly roll-style. Bake on greased baking sheet according to package directions, adding a few minutes to baking time if necessary. Slice to serve.*

Couscous Pilaf Salad

In this great make-ahead salad, crunchy vegetables, peas and raisins add an interesting combination of flavor, color and texture to couscous.

2 tbsp	vegetable oil	25 mL
1	onion, chopped	1
2 tbsp	each cider vinegar and chicken stock	25 mL
1 tbsp	curry powder	15 mL
1 tsp	packed brown sugar	5 mL
1/2 tsp	each salt and ground cumin	2 mL
Pinch	cinnamon	Pinch
2 cups	fresh or frozen peas, cooked	500 mL
1/2 cup	diced sweet red or green pepper	125 mL
1/4 cup	raisins	50 mL

	COUSCOUS	
1 cup	couscous	250 mL
1-1/3 cups	chicken or vegetable stock	325 mL

COUSCOUS: In nonstick skillet, cook couscous over medium heat, stirring frequently, for 5 to 7 minutes or until lightly browned; remove from heat.

❧ In small saucepan, bring chicken stock to boil; add to couscous. Cover and let stand for 5 minutes; fluff with fork.

❧ Meanwhile, in small saucepan, heat oil over medium heat; cook onion, stirring occasionally, for 3 to 5 minutes or until softened. Stir in vinegar, chicken stock, curry powder, sugar, salt, cumin and cinnamon. Add to couscous along with peas, red pepper and raisins; toss gently. *(Salad can be covered and refrigerated for up to 1 day.)* Makes 6 servings.

Bean and Barley Salad

*Today's guidelines for healthy eating rely on plenty of complex carbohydrates and
lots of fiber. What better way to fill the bill than with beans and grains? Any combination of
colored beans works well for taste and presentation.*

1/2 cup	pearl barley	125 mL
1	can (19 oz/540 mL) chick-peas	1
1	can (19 oz/540 mL) red kidney beans	1
1	can (19 oz/540 mL) white kidney beans	1
1/4 cup	chopped green onions	50 mL
1/4 cup	chopped fresh coriander or parsley	50 mL
2	jalapeño peppers, chopped	2
	DRESSING	
1/3 cup	red wine vinegar	75 mL
1	clove garlic, minced	1
1 tsp	salt	5 mL
1/2 tsp	pepper	2 mL
1/2 tsp	ground cumin	2 mL
1/2 cup	extra virgin olive oil	125 mL

In saucepan of 12 cups (3 L) boiling water, cook barley over medium-high heat for 35 to 40 minutes or until tender but firm; drain and rinse under cold water. Drain again and place in serving bowl.

❧ Drain and rinse chick-peas, and red and white kidney beans; drain well and add to bowl. Add onions, coriander and jalapeño peppers.

❧ DRESSING: In small bowl, combine vinegar, garlic, salt, pepper and cumin; gradually whisk in oil. Toss gently with bean mixture. *(Salad can be covered and refrigerated for up to 1 day. Serve at room temperature.)* Makes 6 servings.

Cucumber Salad with Lime Dressing

*Cucumber and onion slices in vinegar are always a refreshing team. A dash of
hot pepper sauce transforms them into an irresistible relish to serve with chicken or cold meats.*

1	English cucumber (or 2 field cucumbers)	1
1/4 cup	lime juice	50 mL
2 tbsp	each vegetable oil, white wine vinegar and water	25 mL
1 tbsp	granulated sugar	15 mL
1/4 tsp	each salt and pepper	1 mL
Dash	hot pepper sauce	Dash
1 cup	sliced onion	250 mL

With fork tines, score cucumber lengthwise. Halve lengthwise (seed if using field cucumbers); slice thinly crosswise. Place in 4-cup (1 L) glass jar.

❧ In small saucepan, stir together lime juice, oil, vinegar, water, sugar, salt, pepper and hot pepper sauce; bring to boil, stirring. Reduce heat and simmer for 2 minutes; pour over cucumber and mix well. Let cool.

❧ Add onion; stir well. Cover with jar lid; refrigerate for 12 hours. *(Salad can be refrigerated for up to 2 days.)* Makes 10 servings.

Green Salad with Walnuts and Swiss Cheese

Sturdy greens are best teamed with cheese and walnuts in this zesty salad. Mix and match curly endive, spinach, iceberg or romaine lettuces.

12 cups	torn salad greens	3 L
1 cup	diced Swiss cheese	250 mL
1/2 cup	walnut halves, toasted	125 mL
2 tbsp	chopped fresh parsley	25 mL
2 tbsp	lemon juice	25 mL
	Salt and pepper	
3 tbsp	walnut oil	50 mL
3 tbsp	extra virgin olive oil	50 mL

In salad bowl, combine salad greens, Swiss cheese, walnuts and parsley.

In small bowl, combine lemon juice, and salt and pepper to taste; gradually whisk in walnut oil and olive oil. Toss with salad to coat well. Makes 6 servings.

Thai Tomato and Cucumber Salad

This simple salad with a wonderful fresh flavor is a great way to use summer's bounty of tomatoes.

3	large tomatoes	3
1	English cucumber (about 12 inches/30 cm)	1
1/2 cup	each chopped fresh parsley, mint and coriander	125 mL
3	green onions, chopped	3
1	Spanish onion, thinly sliced	1
	DRESSING	
3 tbsp	lemon juice	50 mL
2 tbsp	Thai fish sauce	25 mL
1 tbsp	granulated sugar	15 mL
1/2 tsp	salt	2 mL
2	cloves garlic, minced	2
Pinch	hot pepper flakes	Pinch
1/3 cup	vegetable oil	75 mL

Core and cut tomatoes into 1/4-inch (5 mm) thick slices. With fork tines, score cucumber lengthwise; slice thinly. Combine parsley, mint, coriander and green onions.

In large glass bowl, layer half each of the Spanish onion, cucumber and tomatoes, sprinkling half of the parsley mixture evenly between layers. Repeat layers, ending with parsley mixture.

DRESSING: In small bowl, whisk together lemon juice, fish sauce, sugar, salt, garlic and hot pepper flakes until sugar has dissolved; gradually whisk in oil. Pour over salad; marinate at room temperature for 30 minutes or in refrigerator for up to 2 hours. Makes 6 to 8 servings.

TIP: Fish sauce is the soy sauce of Southeast Asia. It is made from fermented fish, so don't be put off by its strong smell. When combined with other ingredients, it blooms subtly.

Summer Harvest Chicken Salad

Here's a deliciously crunchy version of chicken salad that includes a pleasant mix of
Canadian-grown foods. Even the peanuts are produced on land where tobacco used to grow.
You'll need about three whole chicken legs or breasts to make this recipe.

2 cups	cubed (unpeeled) apples	500 mL
1 tbsp	lemon juice	15 mL
2 cups	cubed cooked chicken	500 mL
1 cup	chopped celery	250 mL
1/3 cup	chopped green onions	75 mL
1/3 cup	chopped sweet red pepper	75 mL
1/3 cup	roasted unsalted peanuts	75 mL
1/3 cup	light mayonnaise	75 mL
1/3 cup	plain low-fat yogurt	75 mL

1/4 cup	light sour cream	50 mL
2 tsp	sweet mustard	10 mL
	Salt and pepper	
8	lettuce leaves	8

In bowl, toss apples with lemon juice; add chicken, celery, onions, red pepper and peanuts.

❧ Stir together mayonnaise, yogurt, sour cream and mustard; stir into chicken mixture. Season with salt and pepper to taste. Serve on lettuce. Makes 4 servings.

Warm Lamb Salad

This imaginative main-course salad combines the best of summer flavors with grilled lamb.

12	lamb rib chops, about 1/2 inch (1 cm) thick	12
1-1/2 cups	green beans	375 mL
1 cup	green peas	250 mL
1-1/2 cups	sugar snap peas	375 mL
8 cups	assorted torn salad greens	2 L
1/2 cup	diced roasted sweet red pepper	125 mL
1/2 cup	sliced fennel	125 mL
2 tbsp	each chopped fresh basil and chives	25 mL
1 tbsp	chopped fresh chervil or parsley	15 mL
	DRESSING	
3 tbsp	olive oil	50 mL
3 tbsp	corn oil	50 mL
2 tbsp	minced shallots	25 mL
2 tbsp	red wine vinegar	25 mL
1/4 tsp	each salt and pepper	1 mL

DRESSING: In large bowl, whisk together olive and corn oils, shallots, vinegar, salt and pepper. Spoon 2 tbsp (25 mL) into shallow glass baking dish; add chops, turning to coat. Let stand to marinate for 30 minutes.

❧ Meanwhile, in pot of boiling water, cook green beans and green peas for 3 minutes. Add sugar snap peas; cook for about 2 minutes longer or until vegetables are tender-crisp. Drain well and refresh under cold water; pat dry and place in separate bowl. Add 2 tbsp (25 mL) of the dressing; toss to coat.

❧ Place chops on greased grill over high heat; cook for 3 to 4 minutes per side or until desired doneness. Brush with 2 tbsp (25 mL) of the dressing.

❧ To remaining dressing in bowl, add salad greens, red pepper, fennel, basil, chives and chervil; toss to coat. Mound salad attractively on serving plates. Top with vegetables and chops. Makes 4 servings.

TIP: Broil or grill red peppers, turning often, for about 20 minutes or until blistered and charred. Let cool; peel off blackened skin, seed and chop.

GARDEN LUNCH
MENU

Chilled Tomato Orange Soup | Peach Ice Cream
Crunchy Lobster Rolls | Minty Lemon Iced Tea
Bibb and Cucumber Salad

Chilled Tomato Orange Soup

Tangy fresh orange juice spikes a cool tomato soup. For a change of pace, serve in chilled glass mugs, float orange slices on top and add green onions for stirring.

5	tomatoes, peeled, seeded and chopped	5
2 cups	tomato juice	500 mL
1-1/2 cups	orange juice	375 mL
1 tbsp	tomato paste	15 mL
1	small clove garlic, minced	1
3/4 tsp	ground cumin	4 mL
1/4 tsp	each salt and pepper	1 mL
Dash	hot pepper sauce	Dash
4	green onions, chopped	4
1	orange	1
1/4 cup	sour cream or plain yogurt	50 mL

In large bowl, combine tomatoes, tomato juice, orange juice, tomato paste, garlic, cumin, salt, pepper and hot pepper sauce.

In food processor or blender, purée tomato mixture, in batches, until smooth; return to bowl. Refrigerate for about 2 hours or until chilled. (*Soup can be covered and refrigerated for up to 2 days.*) Stir all but 2 tbsp (25 mL) of the onions into soup.

Peel orange. With sharp knife, cut away outer membrane; cut segments away from inner membranes. Chop if desired. Ladle soup into bowls; garnish with sour cream, orange and remaining onion. Makes 8 servings.

Crunchy Lobster Rolls

Lucky the lunch-bunch who live near the lobster-fishing fleet and can feast on this gorgeous and tasty maritime classic. Most Canadians will settle for frozen canned lobster as a best bet. One large can, with the addition of celery and sweet red pepper for crunch, makes these fabulous but thrifty lobster rolls for eight.

1	can (11.3 oz/320 g) frozen lobster meat, thawed	1
1 cup	chopped celery	250 mL
1/2 cup	chopped sweet red pepper	125 mL
1/3 cup	finely chopped onion	75 mL
2/3 cup	mayonnaise	150 mL
1/2 cup	sour cream	125 mL
2 tbsp	chopped fresh basil or dill	25 mL
1 tbsp	lemon juice	15 mL
Dash	hot pepper sauce	Dash
1	hard-cooked egg, chopped	1
	Salt and pepper	
8	oblong bread rolls, buttered	8
	Leaf lettuce	

Drain lobster meat; squeeze dry and shred into small bowl. Add celery, red pepper and onion. (*Recipe can be prepared to this point, covered and refrigerated for up to 1 day.*)

In large bowl, stir together mayonnaise, sour cream, basil, lemon juice and hot pepper sauce; stir in egg and lobster mixture, tossing to combine. Season with salt and pepper to taste. Line rolls with lettuce; divide lobster mixture among rolls. Makes 8 servings.

TIP: Three pounds (1.5 kg) of lobster, cooked, cooled and picked over, will yield the 2 cups (500 mL) meat necessary for this recipe.

Bibb and Cucumber Salad

Nicely dressed delicate greens scattered with cucumber half-moons make a simple, refreshing salad.

3 tbsp	white wine vinegar	50 mL	6	green onions, chopped	6
2 tsp	Dijon mustard	10 mL		Chopped fresh parsley	
1/2 tsp	dried tarragon	2 mL			
1/4 tsp	salt	1 mL			
Pinch	pepper	Pinch			
1/3 cup	vegetable oil	75 mL			
1	large cucumber	1			
14 cups	torn Bibb or Boston lettuce (about 3 heads)	3.5 L			

In bowl, whisk together vinegar, mustard, tarragon, salt and pepper; gradually whisk in oil.

🍃 Cut cucumber in half lengthwise; slice thinly to make 3 cups (750 mL). Place in salad bowl along with lettuce and onions; toss with dressing. Sprinkle with parsley. Makes 8 servings.

OPEN-FACED SUMMER SANDWICHES

Offer a variety of scrumptious open-faced sandwiches and let guests enjoy an array of flavors.

GRILLED CHICKEN BREAST WITH FRUIT SALSA

🍃 Combine 1 chopped peeled mango or 2 peaches, half sweet red pepper cut into 1-inch (2.5 cm) long strips, 2 tbsp (25 mL) chopped fresh coriander and 2 tbsp (25 mL) lime juice.

🍃 Grill 2 boneless skinless chicken breasts for 5 to 8 minutes per side or until no longer pink inside. Sprinkle with salt and pepper to taste; let cool and cut into 1/3-inch (8 mm) thick slices.

🍃 Cut French stick in half lengthwise, then diagonally slice into 5-inch (12 cm) lengths (or use halved hamburger buns). Spread each of 4 slices with 1 tsp (5 mL) butter or mayonnaise; cover with chicken slices and garnish with salsa. Makes 4 servings.

SMOKED TURKEY WITH ASPARAGUS

🍃 Cook 12 trimmed asparagus spears (about 3/4 lb/375 g) in boiling water for 3 to 5 minutes or until tender-crisp. Refresh under cold water; drain and pat dry.

🍃 Spread 1 tsp (5 mL) butter on each of 4 slices of pumpernickel bread. Cover with 6 oz (175 g) thinly sliced smoked turkey; top with asparagus.

🍃 Mix together 1 tbsp (15 mL) Dijon mustard, 2 tbsp (25 mL) mayonnaise and 1 tbsp (15 mL) milk; drizzle over each sandwich. Makes 4 servings.

GREEK SALAD SANDWICHES

🍃 Cut Armenian flatbread into four 5- x 3-inch (12 x 8 cm) pieces; brush with mixture of 4 tsp (20 mL) olive oil and 1 small crushed clove garlic.

🍃 Cover each with 2 or 3 overlapping slices of tomato, then 3 thin slices red onion rings. Top with 2 tbsp (25 mL) crumbled feta cheese, slices of half a marinated or canned artichoke heart and 3 black Greek-style olives. Sprinkle with salt, pepper and chopped fresh oregano to taste. Makes 4 servings.

Peach Ice Cream

Commercial ice cream will never replace the flavor of real homemade summer-fruit ice cream melting in your mouth. Peach, plum, raspberry or strawberry — it's not hard to make, either in a modern ice-cream machine or just in a cake pan with the help of a blender and your freezer.

6	large peaches (1-1/2 lb/750 g)	6
1/4 cup	granulated sugar	50 mL
	CUSTARD	
3	egg yolks	3
1/3 cup	granulated sugar	75 mL
1 cup	light cream	250 mL
1/2 cup	whipping cream	125 mL
1-1/2 tsp	vanilla	7 mL

CUSTARD: In bowl, whisk egg yolks with sugar for 2 minutes or until pale and thickened; set aside. In heavy saucepan, heat light cream over medium-high heat just until bubbles form around edge; gradually whisk into yolk mixture.

❧ In clean saucepan, cook egg mixture over low heat, stirring constantly, for about 12 minutes or until thick enough to coat back of wooden spoon.

❧ Immediately strain through fine sieve into large bowl. Stir in whipping cream and vanilla. Let cool to room temperature. Place waxed paper directly on surface; refrigerate for at least 2 hours or until chilled, or for up to 24 hours.

❧ Peel and slice peaches. In bowl, combine peaches with sugar; let stand for about 20 minutes or until juicy. In food processor or blender, purée peaches to make about 2 cups (500 mL). Fold into chilled custard.

❧ Freeze in ice-cream maker according to manufacturer's directions. (Or, pour into shallow metal pan; cover and freeze for about 3 hours or until almost firm. Break up mixture and transfer to food processor; purée until smooth. Pour into chilled airtight container; freeze for 1 hour or until firm.) Transfer to refrigerator 30 minutes before serving. Makes 3 cups (750 mL).

VARIATION

❧ RED PLUM ICE CREAM: Omit peach mixture. In saucepan, combine 3 cups (750 mL) sliced (unpeeled) red plums (about 5), 1/4 cup (50 mL) water and 2 tbsp (25 mL) granulated sugar; simmer over low heat for 20 minutes or until tender. Purée, then chill; fold into custard.

TIP: You can add a tablespoon (15 mL) of liqueur to the sugared fruit purée: orange liqueur to peaches, cassis to plums.

Minty Lemon Iced Tea

A refreshing thirst quencher, this classic recipe for iced tea adds the flavor of lemon and mint. Make a batch to keep on hand for leisurely summer sipping.

6	Earl Grey tea bags	6
1/2 cup	granulated sugar	125 mL
1/3 cup	fresh mint leaves	75 mL
8 cups	boiling water	2 L
1	lemon, thinly sliced	1
2 tbsp	lemon juice	25 mL
	Ice cubes	
	Fresh mint sprigs	

Place tea bags, sugar and mint leaves in large measure; pour in boiling water, stirring to dissolve sugar. Let steep for 6 minutes or until desired strength; remove tea bags.

❧ Refrigerate for 8 hours. Strain into serving pitcher. (*Tea can be prepared to this point and refrigerated for up to 3 days.*) Add lemon slices, lemon juice and ice. Garnish with mint sprigs. Makes 8 cups (2 L).

Canadian Living's Family Cookbook

Summer Baked-Fruit Compote

For outstanding flavor, use this colorful fruit to dress up angel food cake,
pound cake slices, ice cream or frozen yogurt. Or spoon into dessert nappies or stemmed glasses
and top with Custard and Yogurt Sauce (recipe, page 129).

3	each peaches, apricots and plums	3
1/4 cup	granulated sugar	50 mL
12	strawberries or cherries	12
1/2 cup	blueberries	125 mL

Peel peaches. Cut peaches, apricots and plums into large chunks and place in 8-inch (2 L) square baking dish; sprinkle with sugar. Bake in 350°F (180°C) oven for 20 minutes.

❧ Stir in strawberries and blueberries; bake for about 10 minutes or until fruit is tender. Stir gently. Let cool to room temperature. (*Compote can be covered and refrigerated for up to 5 days.*) Makes 6 servings.

Chocolate Strawberry Fantasies

A perfect strawberry dessert, these filled berries are delicious enough to appeal to children and elegant enough for adults. Hull berries, if you wish, and use fresh mint as stem and leaves.

2 cups	strawberries	500 mL
8 oz	cream cheese	250 g
1/3 cup	granulated sugar	75 mL
1 tsp	vanilla	5 mL
2 oz	bittersweet or semisweet chocolate, melted and cooled	60 g
2 tbsp	orange liqueur	25 mL
1 tsp	finely grated orange rind	5 mL
1/4 cup	finely chopped pistachios	50 mL
	Tiny mint sprigs (optional)	

Starting at tips of strawberries, make 2 crosswise slits almost to stem ends, without cutting through. Set aside.

❧ In bowl, beat together cream cheese, sugar and vanilla; beat in cooled chocolate, orange liqueur and rind.

❧ Using piping bag, pipe cheese mixture into slits in berries. Sprinkle with pistachios; garnish with mint (if using). Refrigerate until chilled. Makes 6 to 8 servings.

Strawberries with Almond Cream

As a finale to that special dinner, serve freshly picked berries with an almond cream sauce that adds a touch of elegance to a simple dessert.

5 cups	strawberries	1.25 L
1/4 cup	instant dissolving (fruit/berry) sugar	50 mL
1 cup	sour cream	250 mL
2 tbsp	almond liqueur	25 mL

Hull strawberries; slice if large. In sieve set over bowl, sprinkle strawberries with sugar; let stand for 1 hour.

❧ Divide strawberries among dessert dishes. Whisk sour cream and liqueur into juice in bowl; pour over berries. Makes 6 servings.

CINNAMON TORTILLAS WITH STRAWBERRY SALSA

Sweet, tart and minty, this chunky salsa is a great foil for crispy tortillas — perfect for brunch or afternoon tea. Make the salsa first; cover and refrigerate. Serve with freshly baked, crisp tortilla wedges.

❧ *Strawberry Salsa:* Combine 2 cups (500 mL) strawberries, chopped, 1 tbsp (15 mL) chopped fresh mint, 1/2 tsp (2 mL) grated lime rind, 1 tbsp (15 mL) lime juice and 1-1/2 tsp (7 mL) liquid honey. Cover and refrigerate for 1 hour.

❧ *Cinnamon Tortillas:* Melt 2 tbsp (25 mL) butter and brush onto both sides of 4 flour tortillas. Combine 2 tbsp (25 mL) granulated sugar with 3/4 tsp (4 mL) cinnamon; sprinkle over each side of tortillas. Bake on lightly greased baking sheet in 375°F (190°C) oven for about 10 minutes or until crisp and golden. Cut into quarters. Serve with Strawberry Salsa. Makes 4 servings.

SWEET ENDINGS

STRAWBERRY SUNDAE TOPPING: *Drizzle this not-too-sweet sauce over ice cream for a delectable taste treat. Keep several jars stored in a cool, dark dry place for a taste of summer later in the season. Delicious over angel cake wedges or lightly poached peach or pear halves.*

In large heavy saucepan, bring 8 cups (2 L) halved strawberries, 1/4 cup (50 mL) water and 1 tbsp (15 mL) coarsely grated orange rind to boil over medium heat. Reduce heat to medium-low; cover and simmer for 10 minutes. Stir in 1 cup (250 mL) granulated sugar, 1/2 cup (125 mL) corn syrup and 1/2 cup (125 mL) orange juice;

return to boil and boil, uncovered, for 10 minutes, stirring often.

Pour into hot canning jars, leaving 1/4-inch (5 mm) headspace. Seal with lids and screw bands applied firmly without forcing. Process in boiling water bath for 10 minutes. Let cool on rack; check to ensure seal. Makes about 6 cups (1.5 L).

CUSTARD AND YOGURT SAUCE: *Spoon this delicious, rich-tasting sauce over fresh fruit, a baked fruit compote or frozen fruit-flavored yogurt. A lighter version of an old-fashioned dessert sauce, it can be covered and refrigerated for up to three days.*

In saucepan, whisk together 1/2 cup (125 mL) milk and 1-1/2 tsp (7 mL) cornstarch. Whisk in 1 egg yolk and 2 tbsp (25 mL) granulated sugar. Cook over medium heat, stirring constantly, for 3 to 5 minutes or until bubbly and thickened. Remove from heat; stir in 1-1/2 tsp (7 mL) vanilla. Transfer to bowl; place plastic wrap directly on surface. Refrigerate for about 45 minutes or until cool. Stir in 1/2 cup (125 mL) low-fat plain yogurt. Makes about 1 cup (250 mL).

Strawberry Shortcake

Regardless of how you like shortcake — sponge cake or biscuit — you can't miss with this feathery family-size biscuit, split and filled with sugared strawberries, then smothered with whipped cream and more berries.

2 cups	all-purpose flour	500 mL
2 tbsp	granulated sugar	25 mL
1 tbsp	baking powder	15 mL
1/2 tsp	salt	2 mL
1/2 cup	butter	125 mL
1/2 cup	milk or light cream	125 mL
	GLAZE	
1 tsp	milk	5 mL
1 tsp	granulated sugar	5 mL
	STRAWBERRY FILLING	
2 cups	sliced strawberries	500 mL
2 tbsp	(approx) granulated sugar	25 mL
1 tbsp	sherry	15 mL
1 cup	whipping cream	250 mL
6 to 8	whole strawberries	6 to 8

In large bowl, combine flour, sugar, baking powder and salt; with pastry blender or two knives, cut in butter until mixture resembles coarse crumbs. With fork, quickly stir in milk; form into ball.

On lightly floured surface, knead dough 8 to 10 times; shape into 8-inch (20 cm) round about 1/2 inch (1 cm) thick. Place on nonstick baking sheet.

GLAZE: Brush dough with milk; sprinkle with sugar. Bake in 425°F (220°C) oven for 15 to 18 minutes or until golden.

STRAWBERRY FILLING: Meanwhile, in small bowl, gently stir together strawberries, sugar and sherry; let stand for about 20 minutes or until juicy.

Split warm biscuit in half; place bottom on serving plate. Spoon berries over top, reserving juice; place biscuit top on strawberries.

Whip cream; sweeten with more sugar if desired. Spoon onto biscuit top; drizzle with reserved juice. Garnish with whole strawberries. Makes 6 to 8 servings.

Chapter Seven

The HARVEST and HALLOWEEN

After a stroll through autumn's colors, a visit to a roadside farmer's market or a night of trick-or-treating, head indoors and enjoy nature's bounty. It's irresistible.

THANKSGIVING DINNER
MENU

Squash and Apple Soup	Golden Fruit Salsa
Scalloped Potatoes	Parmesan Herb Rolls
Peach-Glazed Baked Ham	Harvest Pumpkin Pie (recipe, page 138)

Squash and Apple Soup

The first signs of the fall harvest, squash and apples are teamed here with a touch of fresh ginger and a hint of brown sugar. Dress up each bowlful with a dollop of yogurt and a sprinkling of pecans.

2 tsp	butter	10 mL
1	onion, chopped	1
1 lb	butternut squash, peeled and chopped	500 g
2	apples, peeled and chopped	2
1	small potato, peeled and chopped	1
1 tsp	grated gingerroot	5 mL
Pinch	white pepper	Pinch
4 cups	water	1 L
1/4 cup	apple cider or juice	50 mL
1 tsp	packed brown sugar	5 mL
1/2 cup	plain yogurt	125 mL
1 tbsp	finely chopped toasted pecans	15 mL

In large saucepan, melt butter over medium heat; cook onion, stirring occasionally, for 4 minutes or until softened.

🍂 Add squash, apples, potato, ginger and pepper; stir in water. Cover and bring to boil; reduce heat and simmer for 12 to 15 minutes or until potato is tender.

🍂 In food processor, purée soup, in batches if necessary, until smooth. Return to saucepan.

🍂 Stir in apple cider and brown sugar; heat to boiling. Ladle into warm soup bowls. Garnish with dollop of yogurt; sprinkle with pecans. Makes 6 servings.

Peach-Glazed Baked Ham

A glazed ham, baked to golden perfection, is a feast for the eyes and the family.

16 lb	fully cooked bone-in ham	7 kg
1/2 cup	peach jam	125 mL
3 tbsp	peach or apricot nectar	50 mL

Remove rind from ham, leaving about 1/4 inch (5 mm) fat. With knife, score fat diagonally in both directions to form diamonds. Place on rack in foil-lined roasting pan; cover with foil. Bake in 325°F (160°C) oven for 3 hours.

❧ Combine jam with nectar; brush some over ham. Bake, uncovered, for 1 hour or until meat thermometer registers 130°F (55°C), brushing with glaze every 20 minutes. Let stand for 10 minutes before carving. Makes 16 to 20 servings.

TIP: For easy slicing, roast the ham a day ahead. Leftovers are a godsend for quick pastas, casseroles, soups or as care packages for returning college students.

Scalloped Potatoes

Prepare this old-fashioned comfort food in the morning, then bake until bubbly and golden at dinnertime.

4 cups	thinly sliced peeled potatoes	1 L
1 cup	water	250 mL
1/2 tsp	salt	2 mL
1 cup	thinly sliced onions (in rings)	250 mL
	Pepper	
2 tbsp	butter	25 mL
2 tbsp	all-purpose flour	25 mL
1-1/2 cups	milk	375 mL
1-1/2 cups	shredded Gouda cheese	375 mL
1 tsp	dried savory	5 mL
Pinch	each cayenne pepper and ground nutmeg	Pinch

In saucepan, bring potatoes, water and salt to boil; cover and cook over medium heat for 7 minutes. Drain well. Arrange one-third of the potatoes over bottom of greased 8-cup (2 L) baking dish; cover with half of the onions. Sprinkle with pepper to taste. Repeat layers. Arrange remaining potatoes over top; set aside.

In small saucepan, melt butter over medium heat; blend in flour and cook, stirring, for 1 minute. Gradually stir in milk and cook, stirring, until thickened. Stir in cheese until melted. Remove from heat; stir in savory, cayenne and nutmeg. Pour evenly over potatoes. *(Casserole can be prepared to this point, cooled in refrigerator and stored for up to 8 hours; add 5 minutes to baking time.)*

Bake in 375°F (190°C) oven for 40 to 45 minutes or until top is golden, sauce is bubbly and potatoes are tender. Let stand for 5 minutes. Makes 4 to 6 servings.

Golden Fruit Salsa

A southwestern-style relish made with peaches or nectarines freshens and updates a traditional ham. It's delicious with chicken, lamb or other cold meats as well.

3 cups	coarsely chopped peeled peaches or unpeeled nectarines	750 mL
3 tbsp	lemon juice	50 mL
1	sweet red pepper, diced	1
4	green onions, sliced	4
2 tbsp	chopped fresh coriander or parsley	25 mL
1/2 tsp	granulated sugar	2 mL
Dash	hot pepper sauce	Dash

In bowl, combine peaches, lemon juice, red pepper, onions, coriander, sugar and hot pepper sauce. Serve immediately or cover and refrigerate for up to 2 hours. Makes about 3-1/2 cups (875 mL).

Parmesan Herb Rolls

Parsley and cheese give character to these store-bought rolls. They even taste homemade.

2	pkg (each 235 g) refrigerator crescent roll dough	2
1/3 cup	freshly grated Parmesan cheese	75 mL
2 tbsp	chopped fresh parsley	25 mL

Unroll dough and separate at perforations; sprinkle with 1/4 cup (50 mL) of the Parmesan and parsley. Starting at short side, roll up and curve to form crescents; place on baking sheets. *(Rolls can be prepared to this point, covered and refrigerated for up to 8 hours.)*

Sprinkle with remaining Parmesan; bake in 375°F (190°C) oven for 10 to 13 minutes or until golden. Remove from pan immediately. Makes 16 rolls.

WHEN TURKEY'S ON THE TABLE

TURKEY TALK

Thanksgiving wouldn't be Thanksgiving to lots of folk without turkey for dinner. We've included a whole plan for cooking the big bird on page 156. But a few reminders at this time of year are in order.

HOW MUCH TO BUY
🍂 A 15-pound (6.75 kg) turkey will serve 8 to 10 people and allows some leftovers.

THAWING THE TURKEY
🍂 *Refrigerator*: Place turkey (in original plastic bag) on tray. Allow 5 hours per pound (10 hours per kilogram).

🍂 *Cold Water*: Cover turkey (in original plastic bag) with cold water, changing water occasionally. Allow 1 hour per pound (2 hours per kilogram).

STUFFING THE TURKEY
🍂 The turkey should never be stuffed ahead of time, but the stuffing can be made ahead and frozen for up to 2 weeks. Frozen stuffing will take 24 hours to thaw in the refrigerator, before stuffing the bird. A 12- to 16-pound (5 to 7 kg) turkey will hold about 5 cups (1.25 L) stuffing in the body cavity and 2 cups (500 mL) in the neck.

THANKSGIVING GARNISHES
🍂 Bunches of herbs (sage, thyme, parsley)
🍂 Orange halves filled with cranberry sauce
🍂 Spiced crab apples and fruit tree leaves
🍂 Dried whole fruit (apricots, figs)
🍂 Thick apple slices sautéed in butter and drizzled with maple syrup
🍂 Brussels sprouts tossed with a little butter and walnut halves or pecans

CRANBERRIES

Crimson cranberries, plump with tartness and firm with flavor, are as traditional to Thanksgiving as turkey. And don't forget them the rest of the year. Cranberries freeze beautifully, and fresh and frozen are interchangeable in recipes. Other ways to use them include:
🍂 Add chopped cranberries to bread stuffing for chicken, turkey, duck and pork.
🍂 Add a few chopped cranberries to cabbage salads or rice.
🍂 Add cranberries to apple or pear crisps and pies.
🍂 Serve leftover cranberry sauce with pancakes, or fold into whipped cream for instant cranberry fool.
🍂 Press cooked cranberries through a sieve and sweeten slightly; serve under grilled breast of chicken.
🍂 Add cranberries to muffins, tea breads, coffee cakes and puddings.
🍂 Mix cranberry juice with white wine or sparkling water for a colorful spritzer.
🍂 Heat cranberry juice with red wine and cinnamon sticks; sweeten with brown sugar to taste.

TRADITIONAL CRANBERRY SAUCE
For the old-fashioned, tried-and-true cranberry sauce with turkey dinner, this is a classic. Perk it up, if you wish, by adding 2 tsp (10 mL) grated orange or lemon rind, or 2 tbsp (25 mL) chopped preserved ginger, before cooking. You can use fresh or frozen cranberries.
🍂 In heavy saucepan, combine 1 cup (250 mL) granulated sugar with 1 cup (250 mL) water; bring to boil. Add 3 cups (750 mL) cranberries; return to boil. Reduce heat and simmer gently until cranberries pop, about 10 minutes. Let cool. (Sauce can be refrigerated in airtight container for up to 1 week). Makes about 2 cups (500 mL).

Peppers Stuffed with Rice, Corn and Tomatoes

Red, yellow or green peppers make colorful containers for this rice stuffing, which is studded with fresh corn and tomatoes, then flavored with tarragon.

3	sweet peppers	3
2 cups	cooked rice	500 mL
3/4 cup	corn kernels	175 mL
3 tbsp	butter, melted	50 mL
2	green onions, chopped	2
1	clove garlic, chopped	1
1	tomato, peeled, seeded and chopped	1
1 tbsp	chopped fresh tarragon or parsley	15 mL
	Salt and pepper	

Halve peppers lengthwise; remove seeds and ribs. In saucepan of boiling salted water, cook peppers for about 5 minutes or until almost tender; drain, pat dry and set aside. In bowl, combine rice with corn; set aside.

🥄 In skillet, heat 1 tbsp (15 mL) of the butter over medium heat; cook onions and garlic, stirring occasionally, for about 3 minutes or just until softened. Stir into rice mixture. Stir in tomato, tarragon, and salt and pepper to taste.

🥄 Spoon rice mixture into pepper halves. Arrange in single layer in greased shallow baking dish; drizzle with remaining butter. (*Peppers can be prepared to this point, covered and refrigerated for up to 24 hours.*)

🥄 Bake in 375°F (190°C) oven for about 20 minutes or until heated through and peppers are tender. Makes 6 servings.

Rutabaga and Pear Purée

*This creamy vegetable purée, delightfully sweetened with pear, can
be made ahead and gently reheated before serving.*

1	small rutabaga or yellow turnip (about 1-1/4 lb/625 g), peeled and cubed	1
1	pear, peeled and cut into chunks	1
1/4 cup	sour cream or plain yogurt	50 mL
1 tbsp	butter	15 mL
Pinch	ground nutmeg	Pinch
	Salt and pepper	

In steamer set over boiling water, steam rutabaga for 15 minutes or until nearly tender. Add pear; steam for 5 to 10 minutes or until rutabaga is tender.

In food processor or blender, purée rutabaga mixture until smooth. *(Purée can be prepared to this point and refrigerated in airtight container for up to 24 hours.)* Add sour cream, butter, nutmeg, and salt and pepper to taste; blend just until combined. Reheat in saucepan over medium-low heat or in microwave until heated through. Makes 4 servings.

Rustic Plum and Nectarine Tart

*Plums and nectarines make a gorgeous filling that tastes as good as it looks.
The juicy flavors are especially good served with whipped cream or custard sauce.*

1/2 cup	(approx) granulated sugar	125 mL
1/3 cup	toasted pecans	75 mL
1/4 cup	all-purpose flour	50 mL
1-1/4 lb	plums (about 14), quartered	625 g
1/2 lb	nectarines (about 3), cut into wedges	250 g
1 tbsp	butter	15 mL
1 tbsp	milk or cream	15 mL
3 tbsp	red currant or sieved apricot jam	50 mL
	PASTRY	
2 cups	all-purpose flour	500 mL
1 tbsp	granulated sugar	15 mL
1/2 tsp	salt	2 mL
1/3 cup	cold butter, cubed	75 mL
1/3 cup	cold lard, cubed	75 mL
1	egg yolk	1
1 tsp	lemon juice	5 mL
	Ice water	

PASTRY: In large bowl, combine flour, sugar and salt; with pastry blender or two knives, cut in butter and lard until in coarse crumbs.

In measuring cup, beat together egg yolk, lemon juice and enough ice water to make 1/2 cup (125 mL); briskly stir enough into flour mixture, 1 tbsp (15 mL) at a time, to make dough hold together.

Shape into disc; wrap and chill for at least 20 minutes. Let cold pastry stand for 15 minutes at room temperature before rolling out.

On lightly floured surface, roll out pastry into 14-inch (35 cm) circle, leaving edges rough. Transfer to 12-inch (30 cm) pizza pan, letting pastry hang over edge.

TIP: You can substitute peaches for the nectarines or make this tart entirely with plums.

In food processor, process half of the sugar, the pecans and flour until nuts are finely ground; sprinkle over pastry. Arrange plums and nectarines over top; sprinkle with remaining sugar. Dot with butter.

Fold pastry overhang over fruit. Brush pastry with milk; sprinkle with a little more sugar. Bake in 425°F (220°C) oven for 15 minutes. Reduce heat to 375°F (190°C); bake for 35 minutes or until bubbly and pastry is golden, shielding crust with foil if necessary. Let cool. Melt jam; brush over fruit. Makes 10 to 12 servings.

*Apple and pumpkin picking is a family affair in the fall.
Dwarf apple trees even let small harvesters get in on the act.*

Harvest Pumpkin Pie

The versatile pumpkin takes a bow throughout the fall season.
Whether this ubiquitous gourd starts a meal or graces your front porch,
it is most memorable as the classic Thanksgiving dessert.

	Pastry for 9-inch (23 cm) double-crust pie (see Perfect Pastry, below)	
2	eggs	2
2 cups	pumpkin purée or 1 can (14 oz/398 mL) pumpkin	500 mL
3/4 cup	packed brown sugar	175 mL
1 tsp	cinnamon	5 mL
1/2 tsp	each ground ginger, allspice and nutmeg	2 mL
1/2 tsp	salt	2 mL
1-1/3 cups	light cream	325 mL
	Sweetened whipped cream	

On lightly floured surface, roll out half of the pastry and fit into 9-inch (23 cm) pie plate. Roll out remaining pastry. Using small maple leaf cookie cutter, cut out leaves. Moisten rim with cold water; arrange pastry leaves around edge, reserving 8 on baking sheet for garnish. Refrigerate pie shell and leaves for 30 minutes.

In bowl, beat eggs lightly; beat in pumpkin, sugar, cinnamon, ginger, allspice, nutmeg and salt. Blend in cream. Pour into prepared pie shell.

Bake pie and reserved pastry leaves in 425°F (220°C) oven for 15 minutes, removing pastry leaves when lightly browned. Reduce heat to 350°F (180°C); bake for about 45 minutes longer or until tester inserted in center comes out clean. Let cool. Garnish with baked pastry leaves. Pipe whipped cream decoratively around leaves. Makes 6 to 8 servings.

Perfect Pastry

A favorite, this pastry can be made by hand or in a food processor.

3 cups	all-purpose flour	750 mL
1 tsp	salt	5 mL
1/2 cup	cold butter, cubed	125 mL
1/2 cup	cold lard or shortening, cubed	125 mL
1	egg	1
2 tsp	white vinegar	10 mL
	Ice water	

In food processor fitted with metal blade, combine flour and salt. Using on/off motion, cut in butter and lard until mixture resembles fine crumbs with a few larger pieces. (Or, in bowl and using pastry blender or two knives, cut butter and lard into flour mixture.)

In measure, beat egg until foamy; add vinegar and enough ice water to make 2/3 cup (150 mL). With motor running, add egg mixture all at once, processing just until dough starts to clump together. Do not let it form ball. (Or, by hand, gradually sprinkle over dry ingredients, tossing with fork until dough holds together.)

Press into 2 discs. Wrap and chill for 30 minutes. (*Dough can be refrigerated for up to 3 days or frozen for up to 3 months; remove from refrigerator 15 minutes before rolling out.*) Makes enough for one 9- or 10-inch (23 or 25 cm) double-crust pie.

Canadian Living's Family Cookbook

Georgian Bay Apple Pie

Serve your guests and family a slice of heaven.

	Pastry for deep 9-inch (23 cm) double-crust pie (see Perfect Pastry, page 138)	
1 tbsp	light cream	15 mL
1 tsp	granulated sugar	5 mL
	FILLING	
8 cups	sliced peeled apples	2 L
3/4 cup	granulated sugar	175 mL
3 tbsp	all-purpose flour	50 mL
2 tsp	coarsely grated orange rind	10 mL
1/4 tsp	ground nutmeg	1 mL
1-1/2 tsp	butter	7 mL
1-1/2 tsp	orange juice	7 mL

On lightly floured surface, roll out half of the pastry and fit into deep 9-inch (23 cm) pie plate; set aside.
❧ FILLING: In large bowl, toss together apples, sugar, flour, orange rind and nutmeg; spoon into pie shell. Dot with butter; sprinkle with orange juice.
❧ Roll out remaining pastry. Moisten rim of shell and fit pastry over filling; trim and crimp edge. Brush with cream; sprinkle with sugar. Cut steam vents in top.
❧ Bake in 425°F (220°C) oven for 20 minutes; reduce heat to 375°F (190°C) and bake for 35 to 40 minutes longer or until apples are tender and pastry is golden. Let cool. Makes 6 to 8 servings.

TIP: Perfect apple pie, like this one, should be filled with lightly spiced, juicy and tender apple slices, and coupled with a flaky pastry that's crisp on the bottom, tender and golden on top. Use Spy or Empire apples for a hard-to-beat pie.

Linda Rice shows off a couple of fresh-baked pies from Goldsmith Orchard near Thornbury, Ontario.

Concord Grape Pie with Orange Pastry

*Only during the fall harvest are Concord grapes available for this
great taste sensation. If you have never tried a pie with blue grapes (and most of us
think of them only for jam and jelly), you're in for a treat.*

5 cups	purple Concord grapes, stemmed	1.25 L
1 cup	granulated sugar	250 mL
2 tbsp	instant tapioca	25 mL
2 tbsp	butter, melted	25 mL
1 tbsp	lemon juice	15 mL
Pinch	ground nutmeg	Pinch
	ORANGE PASTRY	
1-1/2 cups	all-purpose flour	375 mL
1/2 tsp	salt	2 mL
1/4 tsp	grated orange rind	1 mL
3/4 cup	shortening	175 mL
1/4 cup	orange juice	50 mL

ORANGE PASTRY: In bowl, combine flour, salt and orange rind; with pastry blender or two knives, cut in shortening until in coarse crumbs. With fork, gradually mix in orange juice until moistened. Press into ball; flatten into disc, cover lightly and refrigerate for 30 minutes.

⅜ Squeeze each grape to pop pulp from skin; chop skins finely and set aside. In saucepan, cover and cook pulp over medium heat for 5 to 8 minutes or until seeds separate. Pass through food mill or press through strainer to remove seeds. Let cool. Mix pulp with skins, sugar, tapioca, butter, lemon juice and nutmeg.

⅜ On lightly floured surface, roll out two-thirds of the pastry and fit into deep 9-inch (23 cm) pie plate. Trim edge 1/2 inch (1 cm) beyond rim; fold under and flute neatly. Spoon filling into shell.

⅜ Roll out remaining pastry; cut out bunch of grapes and leaves. Arrange over two-thirds of the filling. Bake in 400°F (200°C) oven for 30 to 40 minutes or until pastry is browned and filling is bubbly. Let cool. Makes 6 to 8 servings.

Honey-Glazed Pumpkin Bread

Homemade pumpkin purée makes a wonderfully moist and tender tea bread.
Spread thin slices of this honey-glazed loaf with butter or cream cheese.

1 cup	granulated sugar	250 mL
1 cup	pumpkin purée (see Fresh Pumpkin Purée, page 145)	250 mL
2	eggs	2
1/4 cup	vegetable oil	50 mL
1/4 cup	milk	50 mL
2-1/4 cups	all-purpose flour	550 mL
1/2 cup	ground pecans	125 mL
2 tsp	grated orange rind	10 mL
1-1/2 tsp	baking powder	7 mL
1/2 tsp	baking soda	2 mL
1/2 tsp	cinnamon	2 mL
1/2 tsp	ground ginger	2 mL
1/4 tsp	mace	1 mL
2 tbsp	liquid honey	25 mL

In large bowl, stir sugar with pumpkin; beat in eggs, oil and milk.

❧ Combine flour, pecans, orange rind, baking powder, baking soda, cinnamon, ginger and mace; stir into pumpkin mixture just until moistened.

❧ Pour into greased 9- x 5-inch (2 L) loaf pan; bake in 350°F (180°C) oven for 50 to 60 minutes or until cake tester inserted in center comes out clean.

❧ Brush honey over loaf; let cool in pan on rack for 10 minutes. Loosen sides with metal spatula, remove from pan and let cool on rack. Wrap and store for 1 day before slicing. Makes 1 loaf.

White Wine and Green Grape Sangria

Refreshing sangria pleases fall palates with a
trio of juicy late-harvest fruits — peaches, pears and grapes, of course.

1	each peach and pear	1
1 cup	seedless green grapes	250 mL
2	thin slices lemon	2
1	thin slice orange	1
2 tbsp	granulated sugar	25 mL
4 cups	dry white wine	1 L
	Ice	
2	cans (each 10 oz/284 mL) club soda, chilled	2

Peel and slice peach and pear. In large pitcher, combine peach, pear, grapes, lemon, orange and sugar. Pour in wine; cover and refrigerate for 8 hours.

❧ To serve, place ice in glasses. With slotted spoon, divide fruit mixture among glasses. Fill each three-quarters full with wine mixture. Pour in soda, stirring gently. Serve immediately with spoons for fruit. Makes about 8 servings.

VARIATION

❧ WHITE GRAPE JUICE SANGRIA: Substitute white grape juice for white wine and omit sugar. Add club soda to taste.

Chocolate Chip Hermits

These soft spicy cookies are colorful and moist thanks to the pumpkin.

3/4 cup	shortening	175 mL
1-1/4 cups	packed brown sugar	300 mL
2	eggs	2
1 cup	pumpkin purée (see Fresh Pumpkin Purée, below)	250 mL
1 tsp	vanilla	5 mL
2 cups	all-purpose flour	500 mL
1 tsp	baking powder	5 mL
1 tsp	cinnamon	5 mL
1/2 tsp	baking soda	2 mL
1/2 tsp	salt	2 mL
1/2 tsp	each ground nutmeg, allspice and cloves	2 mL
1 cup	raisins	250 mL
1 cup	chocolate chips	250 mL
1/2 cup	chopped dates	125 mL
1/2 cup	chopped nuts	125 mL

In large bowl, beat together shortening and sugar; beat in eggs, pumpkin and vanilla.

❧ Combine flour, baking powder, cinnamon, baking soda, salt, nutmeg, allspice and cloves; stir into sugar mixture. Stir in raisins, chocolate chips, dates and nuts.

❧ Drop by rounded teaspoonfuls (5 mL) onto greased baking sheets. Bake in 350°F (180°C) oven for 10 to 12 minutes or until golden brown. Makes about 60 cookies.

AFTER THE JACK-O-LANTERN...WHAT?

Pumpkin seeds make a terrific snack. And while pumpkins are such a good price, why not make pumpkin purée.

ROASTED PUMPKIN SEEDS
❧ Rinse pumpkin seeds under cold running water, discarding strings. Spread 2 cups (500 mL) in single layer on two baking sheets. Let dry thoroughly, stirring once or twice to separate and turn.
❧ In small bowl, combine seeds with 2 tsp (10 mL) vegetable oil and 1/4 tsp (1 mL) salt, stirring to coat well; spread on baking sheets.
❧ Bake in 375°F (190°C) oven, stirring and spreading once, for 15 to 20 minutes or until deep golden brown. Let cool. Store in airtight container. Makes 2 cups (500 mL).

FRESH PUMPKIN PURÉE
❧ One pound (500 g) raw pumpkin yields about 1 cup (250 mL) purée.
❧ Cut pumpkin in half. Remove seeds and stringy fibers. Cut pumpkin into large chunks.

Steam until tender. Or, place pieces, skin side up, in jelly roll pan; pour in water to depth of 1/2 inch (1 cm). Bake in 350°F (180°C) oven for about 1 hour or until tender.
❧ Scrape pulp away from rind; drain pulp thoroughly. Purée pulp in food processor or pass through food mill; drain in sieve for 15 minutes.
❧ Cover and refrigerate purée for up to 1 week or freeze for up to 6 months.

CARVE A PUMPKIN WITH PERSONALITY

Make your own happy face, monster glare or toothless wonder to light up your house on All Hallows' Eve (better known today as Halloween).
❧ Cut a lid, leaving stem in place; cut three air vents in the lid.

❧ Scrape out pulp and seeds, leaving 1-inch (2.5 cm) thick shell.
❧ With felt marker, outline eyes, nose, mouth — anything you plan to cut. Little hands need help with the actual cutting.
❧ Use carrots, parsnips, celery for ears. Celery leaves make great

hair when tucked in between shell and lid.
❧ Candle will stay in center if you light it, then let melted wax drip into a pool in the center of the inside bottom. Quickly stand candle in melted wax and hold until it hardens in place.
❧ Light candle and replace lid.

THRILL THE KIDS ON HALLOWEEN

Have the spookiest Halloween ever this year. You can give the kids (and adults) in your neighborhood a real thrill by taking a few minutes to turn your front porch into a witch's den. Here's what to do.

ᕀ Replace your front porch light with an eerie green or orange bulb.

ᕀ Post signs in the driveway bearing messages such as: Beware of Goblins, Spiders for Sale.

ᕀ Splurge and buy several small pumpkins to place on lampposts, the front steps, the gate. Small warming candles (preferably scented) in each make a moody scene in the front yard.

ᕀ For a final touch, record some spooky sounds to play on Halloween night. A piece of sheet metal vibrates when you shake it, sounding like thunder. Water sprayed from the garden hose onto metal pails sounds like torrential rain. Add a bloodcurdling screech and some loud cackling and you'll have the most popular house on the street to greet trick-or-treaters.

CREATE A COSTUME

Line up the kids this Halloween and create a fabulous face with homemade makeup.

GHASTLY GHOST

ᕀ For white makeup, stir 2 tbsp (25 mL) cornstarch with 1 tbsp (15 mL) shortening until smooth. Apply this makeup to the face, avoiding eye area. Apply and smudge grey eye shadow around eyes. Dust face with cornstarch.

ᕀ In center of white twin-size flat sheet, cut hole the size of the child's face. Place sheet over child's head so face peeks out hole. Tie 40 m white elastic loosely around neck so sheet fits around head like scarf. Put on long white gloves.

Crackling Candy Apples

Crunch through the neon red candy coating into the juicy whiteness of a freshly picked apple.

8	small red apples (preferably McIntosh, Spartan or Cortland)	8
2 cups	granulated sugar	500 mL
1 cup	water	250 mL
1/2 cup	corn syrup	125 mL
1/4 tsp	red food coloring	1 mL

Remove stem from each apple; insert wooden stir stick for holding in center of stem end. Set aside. Grease baking sheet; set aside.

❧ In 12-cup (3 L) heavy saucepan, combine sugar, water and corn syrup; cook, stirring, over medium-low heat for 8 minutes or until sugar has dissolved.

❧ Increase heat to medium-high and bring to boil, brushing down side of pan occasionally with brush dipped in hot water to prevent crystallization. Boil, brushing down side occasionally but not stirring, for 15 to 25 minutes or until at soft-crack stage of 290°F (143°C) on candy thermometer, or until 1/2 tsp (2 mL) syrup dropped into cold water separates into hard but pliable threads.

❧ Remove from heat; immediately stir in food coloring. Immediately plunge bottom of pan into ice water and hold for about 15 seconds or until sizzling stops.

❧ Holding each apple by wooden stick and tilting saucepan, swirl apple in syrup until coated all over.

❧ Lift apple and quickly swirl over pan to allow excess to drip off. Place on prepared baking sheet; let stand at room temperature for at least 30 minutes or until hardened. (*Apples can be stored, loosely covered with plastic wrap, for up to 2 days at room temperature.*) Makes 8 servings.

VARIATION

❧ CARAMEL APPLES: Increase apples to 10. Substitute whipping cream for water and brown sugar for granulated sugar. Cook until hard-ball stage of 258°F (125°C) on candy thermometer, or until hard ball forms when dropped into cold water. When cooling pan in ice water, stir caramel with wooden spoon until smooth. Turn each apple in caramel 4 or 5 times or until well coated. Makes 10 servings.

TIP: Watch the boiling sugar mixture carefully, because the temperature rises quickly near the end of the cooking process and the mixture burns easily. Plunging the pan into ice water stops the cooking and prevents burning. Wear rubber gloves when swirling the apples to avoid sugar burns.

Caramel Corn

*A sure hit for a Halloween treat or warm from the oven as a family snack,
this caramel corn is a cinch to make — and delicious!*

1 cup	granulated sugar	250 mL
1 cup	packed brown sugar	250 mL
1 cup	butter	250 mL
1/2 cup	corn syrup	125 mL
Pinch	cream of tartar	Pinch
1 tsp	baking soda	5 mL
20 cups	freshly popped popcorn (about 1 cup/250 mL popping corn)	5 L

In heavy saucepan, stir together granulated and brown sugars, butter, corn syrup and cream of tartar; bring to boil, stirring. Boil for 5 minutes without stirring; remove from heat. Stir in baking soda.

🍂 Place popcorn in roasting pan; pour sugar mixture over top and stir to coat well. Bake in 200°F (100°C) oven for 1 hour, stirring every 10 minutes. Let cool, stirring occasionally. Store in airtight containers. Makes 20 cups (5 L).

Molasses Pulled Taffy

This old-fashioned pulled taffy has always been a Halloween treat. French-Canadian children traditionally make "tire à la mélasse" on November 25, the feast day of St. Catherine. Years ago, unmarried women of 25 were also expected to wear the starched cap of the spinster on this day. Thank goodness the cap has disappeared, but the pulled taffy remains!

1-1/4 cups	packed brown sugar	300 mL
1/3 cup	fancy molasses	75 mL
1/4 cup	water	50 mL
2 tbsp	cider vinegar	25 mL
2 tsp	butter	10 mL
1/4 tsp	baking soda	1 mL

In large heavy saucepan, combine sugar, molasses, water, vinegar and butter; bring to boil, stirring until sugar has dissolved. Boil, without stirring and brushing down side of pan occasionally with brush dipped in hot water, until at soft-crack stage of 270°F (132°C) on candy thermometer, or until 1/2 tsp (2 mL) syrup dropped into cold water separates into hard but pliable threads. Remove from heat. Immediately stir in baking soda.

🍂 Pour onto greased rimmed baking sheet; let cool for 3 minutes. With metal spatula, fold over edges until cool enough to handle. Candy is ready to pull when hole poked in center holds its shape.

🍂 With buttered hands, gather taffy into ball and pull, folding ends together. Continue pulling and folding until taffy is golden and satiny.

🍂 Between two people, twist and pull until taffy is evenly stretched to about 1/2-inch (1 cm) thickness. Cut into pieces while still supple. Wrap in waxed paper. Makes 45 to 50 pieces.

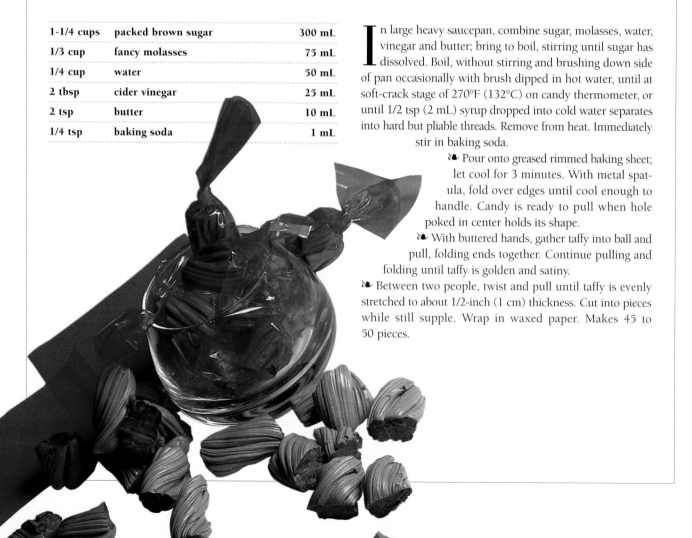

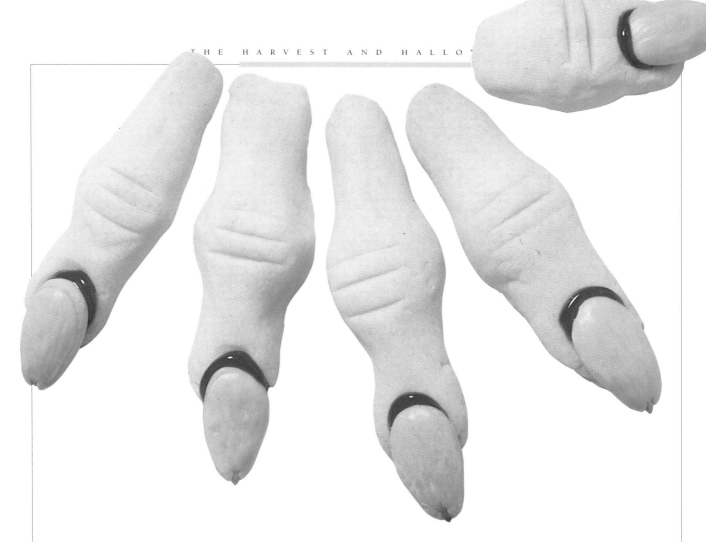

Witch's Fingers

Sometimes even cookies as creepy as these are so delicious you just have to try a batch!
After Halloween, make them plain, without the nails and knuckles.

1 cup	butter, softened	250 mL
1 cup	icing sugar	250 mL
1	egg	1
1 tsp	almond extract	5 mL
1 tsp	vanilla	5 mL
2-3/4 cups	all-purpose flour	675 mL
1 tsp	baking powder	5 mL
1 tsp	salt	5 mL
3/4 cup	whole blanched almonds	175 mL
1	tube (19 g) red decorator gel	1

In bowl, beat together butter, sugar, egg, almond extract and vanilla; beat in flour, baking powder and salt. Cover and refrigerate for 30 minutes.

❧ Working with one-quarter of the dough at a time and keeping remaining dough refrigerated, roll heaping teaspoonful (5 mL) into finger shape. Press almond firmly into 1 end for nail. Press in center to create knuckle shape. Using paring knife, make slashes in several places to form knuckle.

❧ Bake on lightly greased baking sheets in 325°F (160°C) oven for 20 to 25 minutes or until pale golden. Let cool for 3 minutes.

❧ Lift up almond; squeeze red decorator gel onto nail bed and press almond back in place, so gel oozes out from underneath. Remove from baking sheets; let cool on racks. Makes about 60 cookies.

Spicy Apple Drink

*Sweet enough to tickle the palates of most children, this is also a good adult
warmer-upper after an evening of trick-or-treating. Garnish each mugful with one of the orange slices.*

8	whole cloves	8
2	sticks cinnamon	2
1/4 tsp	ground nutmeg	1 mL
5 cups	apple cider	1.25 L
2 tbsp	packed brown sugar	25 mL
1	orange, thinly sliced	1
Half	lemon, thinly sliced	Half

In small square of cheesecloth, tie together cloves, cinnamon and nutmeg.

🍂 In 8-cup (2 L) microwaveable measure, combine cider, sugar, orange, lemon and spice bag; cover and microwave at High for 8 to 9 minutes or until boiling. Stir; let stand, covered, for 5 minutes. Remove bag; strain into mugs. Makes 4 servings.

TIP: This drink is just as easy to bring to boil on the stovetop, then stir and let stand for 5 minutes before straining into mugs.

Ghoulade

The name makes you shiver, but this is the kind of drink that has kid-appeal. Tastes refreshing, too.

1	can (16-2/3 oz/474 mL) frozen unsweetened orange juice concentrate	1
2	cans (each 275 mL) frozen cranberry juice concentrate	2
8 cups	pineapple juice	2 L
3	bottles (each 1 L) ginger ale	3
	Frozen raspberries	

In large plastic container, let orange and cranberry concentrates soften; stir in pineapple juice until blended. Freeze until solid.

🍂 Place 2 scoops of frozen juice mixture in each glass; fill with ginger ale. Add a few raspberries. Makes 24 servings.

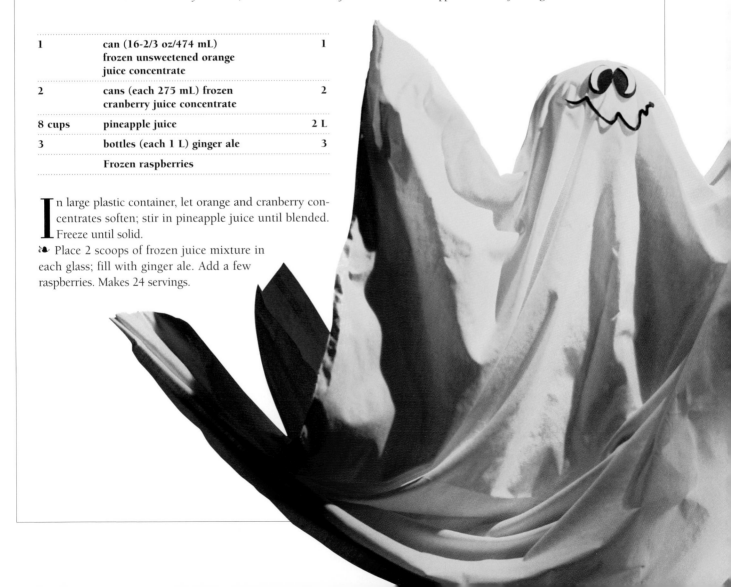

Chapter Eight

The HOLIDAYS are HERE

Merry Christmas!
Happy Hannukah! Season's Greetings!
Warm hearth and home with
old and new favorites from the kitchen.

MAKE-AHEAD CHRISTMAS FEAST
MENU

Two-Mushroom Consommé*

Turkey with Fruited Nut
and Rice Stuffing*

Cranberry Sauce (recipe, page 134)

Fluffy Mashed Potatoes

Maple Walnut Squash Purée*

Green Peas with Onion and Mint

Mixed Greens with Basil Vinaigrette

Buttermilk Parsley Rolls*

Holiday Plum Pudding with
Warm Brandied Sauce*

Recipes included

Two-Mushroom Consommé

Dried mushrooms intensify the delicate flavor of this elegant soup.

1/2 oz	dried wild mushrooms (porcini, morels or shiitake)	15 g
2 tbsp	vegetable oil	25 mL
3 cups	sliced fresh mushrooms	750 mL
6	green onions, diagonally sliced	6
6 cups	chicken stock	1.5 L
	Salt and pepper	

Rinse dried mushrooms and place in bowl. Pour in 1 cup (250 mL) boiling water; soak for 15 minutes. Strain through cheesecloth-lined sieve, reserving liquid. Rinse mushrooms again; chop coarsely. Set aside.

🍂 In saucepan, heat oil over medium heat; cook fresh mushrooms and half of the onions, stirring occasionally, for about 5 minutes or until liquid has evaporated.

🍂 Add stock and reserved dried mushrooms and liquid; bring to boil. Reduce heat and simmer for 15 minutes. Season with salt and pepper to taste. *(Soup can be cooled in refrigerator, covered and stored for up to 3 days; reheat over medium-low heat.)* Sprinkle each serving with remaining onions. Makes 8 servings.

Buttermilk Parsley Rolls

Tender parsley-flecked rolls are easily made with quick-rising (instant) yeast.
Buttering the tops adds a glisten and softens the crusts. These can be made ahead,
frozen and reheated while the turkey is standing. (Photo, page 152)

4 cups	(approx) all-purpose flour	1 L
1	pkg (8 g) quick-rising (instant) dry yeast	1
1/4 cup	chopped fresh parsley	50 mL
1 tsp	granulated sugar	5 mL
1-1/2 tsp	salt	7 mL
1/2 tsp	baking soda	2 mL
1 cup	buttermilk	250 mL
1/2 cup	water	125 mL
1/4 cup	butter	50 mL
2 tbsp	butter, melted (optional)	25 mL

In bowl, combine 3 cups (750 mL) of the flour, yeast, parsley, sugar, salt and baking soda. Heat buttermilk, water and butter until 125°F (50°C) or hot to the touch (mixture may curdle). Whisk buttermilk mixture; stir into flour mixture. Stir in enough of the remaining flour to make soft dough.

🍂 Turn out onto lightly floured surface; knead for about 8 minutes or until smooth and elastic. Cover and let rest for 10 minutes.

🍂 Divide dough into 12 pieces; shape into balls, pinching at bottom to seal. Place balls, seam side down, in bottomless 10-inch (3 L) springform pan set on baking sheet. Cover and let rise in warm place until doubled in bulk, about 45 minutes.

🍂 Bake in 375°F (190°C) oven for 15 to 20 minutes or until golden and hollow-sounding when tapped on bottom. Remove from pan and let cool on rack. *(Rolls can be wrapped and frozen for up to 2 weeks; thaw, wrap in foil and reheat in 400°F/200°C oven for 10 to 15 minutes or until warmed through.)* Brush tops with melted butter (if using). Makes 12 rolls.

Turkey with Fruited Nut and Rice Stuffing

Memories of Christmas always include the special feast with family and friends. Traditional turkey wins with timed-to-perfection roasting, a moist fruity stuffing and rich brown gravy.

For eight servings, a 12-lb (5.5 kg) turkey will be perfect. Remove giblets and neck from turkey; set aside for Giblet Stock.

🍂 Rinse turkey inside and out; dry skin and cavity well. Loosely fill neck opening and body cavity with stuffing (recipe follows); skewer closed. Place on rack in roasting pan. Rub with 1/4 cup (50 mL) softened butter and 1 tsp (5 mL) dried thyme. Sprinkle with salt and pepper.

🍂 Tent with foil and roast in 325°F (160°C) oven for 3 hours, basting if desired. Remove foil and roast, basting if desired, for 1 hour longer or until golden brown and meat thermometer inserted in thigh reads 185°F (85°C) and in stuffing 165°F (75°C). Let stand on platter, lightly covered, for 20 minutes before carving.

TIP: If you plan to serve more than eight people, or want to indulge in plenty of leftovers, choose at least a 15-pound (6.25 kg) turkey and increase roasting time to about four hours.

FRUITED NUT AND RICE STUFFING

2 tbsp	butter	25 mL
2	onions, chopped	2
2	stalks celery, chopped	2
3/4 tsp	dried thyme	4 mL
1	bay leaf	1
1 cup	wild rice, rinsed	250 mL
3-1/2 cups	chicken stock	875 mL
1-1/2 cups	parboiled rice	375 mL
3/4 cup	chopped dried apricots	175 mL
3/4 cup	chopped toasted almonds	175 mL
1/4 cup	chopped fresh parsley	50 mL
1/4 tsp	each salt and pepper	1 mL

🍂 In Dutch oven, melt butter over medium heat; cook onions, celery, thyme and bay leaf, stirring occasionally, for 5 minutes or until softened.

🍂 Stir in wild rice; add stock and bring to boil. Reduce heat to low; cover and simmer for 20 minutes.

🍂 Add parboiled rice; cook, covered, for 15 to 20 minutes or until rice is tender and liquid absorbed. Discard bay leaf.

🍂 Stir in apricots, almonds, parsley, salt and pepper. Let cool completely. *(Stuffing can be refrigerated in airtight container for up to 2 days or frozen for up to 2 weeks; thaw in refrigerator for 48 hours.)* Makes about 8 cups (2 L).

TIP: If you're fortunate enough to have extra stuffing after filling the bird, place it in a greased casserole and drizzle with 1/2 cup (125 mL) stock; heat in 400°F (200°C) oven for 25 to 30 minutes.

Pan Gravy

Foolproof and delicious, this easy gravy adds the crowning touch to a memorable Christmas bird.

	Pan drippings from turkey	
3 tbsp	all-purpose flour	50 mL
2 cups	Giblet Stock (recipe follows)	500 mL
	Salt and pepper	

Skim off fat from drippings in roasting pan. Stir flour into pan drippings; cook, stirring, over medium heat for 1 minute.

🍂 Whisk in stock and bring to boil, stirring to scrape up brown bits. Reduce heat and simmer for 5 minutes. Season with salt and pepper to taste. Strain if desired. Makes 2 cups (500 mL).

GIBLET STOCK

6 cups	water	1.5 L
1	onion, chopped	1
1	carrot, chopped	1
1	stalk celery, chopped	1
	Turkey giblets, heart and neck	

🍂 In saucepan, combine water, onion, carrot, celery and turkey parts; bring to boil. Reduce heat to low and skim off fat; cook for 3 hours. Strain into measuring cup to make 2 cups (500 mL). *(Stock can be covered and refrigerated for up to 1 day.)* Makes 2 cups (500 mL).

COUNTDOWN TO CHRISTMAS DINNER

The big Christmas feast will be just as glorious — and a lot easier on the cook — if it's done in stages. Get a two-week head start and follow our plan. Then, on Christmas Day, as roasting turkey fills the house with its unforgettable aroma, family and friends can help you put the best dinner of the year on the table.

TWO WEEKS AHEAD
Make and freeze
- Maple Walnut Squash Purée
- Fruited Nut and Rice Stuffing
- Buttermilk Parsley Rolls
- Holiday Plum Pudding

THREE DAYS AHEAD
- Make and refrigerate Two-Mushroom Consommé
- Place frozen turkey in refrigerator to thaw
- Make cranberry sauce (recipe, page 134)

ONE DAY AHEAD
- Thaw stuffing in refrigerator
- Set table
- Make centerpiece
- Place juices, mixes and wine in refrigerator to chill
- Wash salad greens and wrap in towels; place in plastic bag and refrigerate
- Toast walnuts for squash purée
- Make Giblet Stock
- Thaw Plum Pudding
- Make Vanilla Hard Sauce

ON THE BIG DAY
- Thaw rolls in morning
- Prepare turkey; stuff and roast
- Make Warm Brandied Sauce
- Remove squash purée from refrigerator 30 minutes before reheating
- Peel, cook and mash potatoes; keep warm
- Place condiments in dishes
- Reheat Plum Pudding
- Reheat consommé
- Remove turkey from oven
- Reheat squash purée and any extra rice stuffing
- Reheat rolls
- Heat peas
- Make gravy
- Carve turkey
- Toss salad with dressing
- Garnish turkey platter with parsley and thyme sprigs, whole dried apricots and almonds in shells
- Add chopped walnuts to Maple Walnut Squash Purée in an interesting pattern — strips, circle, zigzags
- Reheat Warm Brandied Sauce

Maple Walnut Squash Purée

Lightly sweetened with maple syrup, this make-ahead dish can also be served right away. Garnish with walnuts before serving. (Photo, page 152)

12 cups	cubed peeled squash	3 L
3 tbsp	butter	50 mL
3 tbsp	maple syrup	50 mL
3/4 tsp	salt	4 mL
1/4 tsp	each ground nutmeg and pepper	1 mL
1/4 cup	chopped walnuts, toasted	50 mL

In large pot of boiling salted water, cook squash for 25 minutes or until tender; drain. Purée in food processor or blender until smooth; blend in butter, maple syrup, salt, nutmeg and pepper.

- Spoon squash mixture into shallow greased 8-cup (2 L) casserole or baking dish; garnish with walnuts. Serve immediately. Makes 8 servings.

TIP: To make purée ahead of time, omit walnuts, cover and refrigerate for up to 2 days. Or, freeze for up to 2 weeks; thaw in refrigerator for 3 days. Remove from refrigerator 30 minutes before baking, covered, in 400°F (200°C) oven for 25 minutes. Garnish with walnuts; bake, uncovered, for 10 minutes or until heated through. To toast walnuts for extra flavor, cook in small skillet over medium heat, stirring, for about 5 minutes.

Holiday Plum Pudding

Fruit-filled and spicy, this pudding is reminiscent of the wonderful flavors
found in family recipes from British settlers. Serve with Warm Brandied Sauce and Vanilla Hard Sauce.

2 cups	fine fresh bread crumbs	500 mL
1/2 cup	hot milk	125 mL
3 oz	ground suet	75 g
3	eggs, beaten	3
1/2 cup	packed brown sugar	125 mL
1/2 cup	molasses	125 mL
1/2 cup	strawberry jam	125 mL
1 tbsp	grated orange rind	15 mL
1/4 cup	orange juice	50 mL
1 tsp	grated lemon rind	5 mL
2 tbsp	lemon juice	25 mL
1/2 tsp	salt	2 mL
1/2 tsp	each cinnamon, ground cloves and nutmeg	2 mL
3/4 cup	each lexia raisins and sultana raisins	175 mL
3/4 cup	each chopped dates and figs	175 mL
3/4 cup	halved red candied cherries	175 mL
3/4 cup	diced candied pineapple	175 mL
3/4 cup	mixed candied peel	175 mL

In bowl, stir bread crumbs into milk; let cool. In large bowl, whisk together suet, eggs, sugar, molasses, jam, orange rind and juice, lemon rind and juice, salt, cinnamon, cloves and nutmeg. Whisk in bread mixture. Stir in lexia and sultana raisins, dates, figs, cherries, pineapple and candied peel, mixing well.

❧ Spoon into 8-cup (2 L) greased heatproof pudding mould. Make wide pleat in large piece of waxed paper; place over mould. Cover with enough foil to press down side of mould; tie string tightly around mould.

❧ Place on rack in large saucepan; pour in enough boiling water to come two-thirds up sides. Cover and simmer over medium heat, adding water as needed to maintain level, for about 4 hours or until cake tester inserted in center comes out clean.

❧ Let stand for 15 minutes. Remove foil and paper; unmould onto serving plate. *(Pudding can be wrapped and refrigerated for up to 2 months or frozen for longer storage. To reheat, return to mould, cover and steam for 1 to 1-1/2 hours.)* Makes 8 to 10 servings.

Vanilla Hard Sauce

In bowl, beat 1/4 cup (50 mL) softened butter until fluffy; gradually beat in 1 cup (250 mL) sifted icing sugar until blended. Blend in 1 tsp (5 mL) vanilla. Transfer to serving bowl. Cover and refrigerate until chilled. Garnish with candied cherries. Makes about 3/4 cup (175 mL).

Warm Brandied Sauce

You can substitute 1 tsp (5 mL) rum extract or brandy extract in place of brandy.

1 cup	water	250 mL
1/4 cup	granulated sugar	50 mL
1 tbsp	cornstarch	15 mL
2 tbsp	butter	25 mL
2 tbsp	brandy	25 mL
1 tsp	vanilla	5 mL
Pinch	salt	Pinch

In saucepan over medium-high heat, stir together water, sugar and cornstarch for 3 to 4 minutes or until boiling and thickened. Remove from heat.

❧ Stir in butter, brandy, vanilla and salt. Makes about 2 cups (500 mL).

Panpepato

*This is a Roman Christmas favorite, filled with fruit and nuts, sweetened with honey and wine,
and dark with chocolate. Shaped by hand, these cakes bake without pans.*

2 cups	all-purpose flour	500 mL
1 tbsp	unsweetened cocoa powder	15 mL
1/2 tsp	each pepper and ground nutmeg	2 mL
1/4 tsp	cinnamon	1 mL
2-1/2 cups	each whole unblanched almonds and hazelnuts	625 mL
2-1/2 cups	chopped walnuts	625 mL
1-1/2 cups	golden raisins	375 mL
1-1/4 cups	candied fruit	300 mL
2/3 cup	minced orange rind (10 oranges)	150 mL
1 cup	liquid honey	250 mL
1/2 cup	granulated sugar	125 mL
1/4 cup	dry white wine	50 mL
3 oz	semisweet chocolate, melted	90 g
	Icing sugar	

In small bowl, blend flour, cocoa, pepper, nutmeg and cinnamon; set aside. In separate bowl, combine almonds, hazelnuts, walnuts, raisins, candied fruit and orange rind; set aside.

🍃 In large saucepan, bring honey, sugar and wine to boil; reduce heat and simmer for 2 minutes. Remove from heat; stir in chocolate. Blend in flour mixture, then nut mixture.

🍃 Divide into 3 portions; place each on piece of waxed paper. With wet hands, shape into 10- x 4-inch (25 x 10 cm) logs, pressing to break air bubbles and pushing in any exposed nuts. Peel off paper; place on greased baking sheet.

🍃 Place in cold oven; turn to 350°F (180°C) and bake for 40 minutes or until lightly browned. Let cool for 10 minutes; let cool completely on racks. Wrap in plastic wrap and foil; let stand for 24 hours. *(Cakes can be stored for up to 1 month.)* To serve, sift icing sugar over top. Makes 3 cakes.

Christmas Fig Cake

*Dried fruit and nuts are simmered in honey and Portuguese brandy, then mellowed
for 24 hours before being baked into a luscious, colorful cake.*

1/4 cup	each rye whisky, port and cherry liqueur	50 mL
1/4 cup	Agua Ardente or other brandy	50 mL
2 tbsp	liquid honey	25 mL
1 cup	each chopped dried figs and raisins	250 mL
1 cup	each chopped candied fruit and walnuts	250 mL
2 cups	granulated sugar	500 mL
1 cup	butter, melted and cooled	250 mL
5	eggs	5
2-2/3 cups	all-purpose flour	650 mL
1 tbsp	baking powder	15 mL
2 tsp	ground nutmeg	10 mL
	Icing sugar	

One day ahead, in saucepan, bring whisky, port, liqueur, Agua Ardente and honey to boil. Add figs, raisins, candied fruit and walnuts; simmer for 5 minutes. Let cool completely. Cover and let stand for 24 hours.

🍃 Grease 10-inch (4 L) tube pan; line base with waxed paper and grease paper. Set aside.

🍃 In large bowl, beat sugar with butter. Beat in eggs, one at a time, beating well after each addition. Beat for 2 minutes or until slightly thickened.

🍃 Blend together flour, baking powder and nutmeg; with wooden spoon, gradually stir into batter until blended. Stir in fruit mixture; scrape into prepared pan.

🍃 Bake in 350°F (180°C) oven, covering with foil if browning too quickly, for about 1 hour and 10 minutes or until top is firm and brown and cake tester inserted in center comes out clean. Let cool completely in pan on rack. Remove from pan; wrap well in plastic wrap and refrigerate for 24 hours. *(Cake can be refrigerated for up to 1 month; sprinkle with more Agua Ardente if cake starts to dry out.)* To serve, sift icing sugar over top. Makes 1 cake.

Panpepato

Canadian Living's Family Cookbook

Apple and Cranberry Pie in Phyllo

*This pie tastes sensational
and it's a lot easier to make than it looks.*

8 cups	sliced peeled apples (Golden Delicious or Empire)	2 L
1 cup	fresh cranberries	250 mL
1/2 cup	packed brown sugar	125 mL
1/4 cup	all-purpose flour	50 mL
1/2 tsp	cinnamon	2 mL
Pinch	ground nutmeg	Pinch
8	sheets phyllo pastry	8
1/2 cup	(approx) butter, melted	125 mL
1/4 cup	dry bread crumbs	50 mL
1/4 cup	finely chopped walnuts	50 mL
	Icing sugar	

In bowl, combine apples, cranberries, brown sugar, flour, cinnamon and nutmeg; set aside.

ᔰ Place 1 sheet of phyllo on work surface, keeping remaining phyllo covered with damp towel to prevent drying out. Brush sheet lightly with butter.

ᔰ Combine bread crumbs with walnuts; sprinkle heaping teaspoonful (5 mL) over one half crosswise. Fold opposite half over top. Brush both sides lightly with butter.

ᔰ Place 1 short end of filled pastry in center of 10-inch (3 L) springform pan, leaving other end to hang over edge. Sprinkle heaping teaspoonful (5 mL) of the walnut mixture over pastry in pan. Repeat with remaining phyllo, overlapping each sheet slightly when arranging in pan to cover bottom of pan completely.

ᔰ Spoon apple filling into pan. Fold overhanging pastry, 1 sheet at a time, over filling to cover. Bake on lowest rack in 400°F (200°C) oven for 15 minutes; reduce heat to 350°F (180°C) and bake, covering loosely with foil to avoid browning too quickly, for 50 to 55 minutes or until apples are tender when pierced with knife. Let cool on rack; remove side of pan. Dust with icing sugar. Makes 8 to 10 servings.

*(clockwise from left) Apple and Cranberry Pie in Phyllo,
Chocolate Brownie Turtle Cake and Triple Lemon Roll*

Triple Lemon Roll

Sweet and tart flavors are beautifully balanced in this fabulous jelly roll dessert.
Lemon appears three times: in the cake, in the syrup and in the filling.

1/3 cup	ground toasted hazelnuts (see Tip, this page)	75 mL
1/4 cup	sifted cake-and-pastry flour	50 mL
1 tsp	grated lemon rind	5 mL
4	eggs, separated	4
2/3 cup	granulated sugar	150 mL
1 tsp	vanilla	5 mL
1/4 tsp	cream of tartar	1 mL
	Sifted icing sugar	
	LEMON SYRUP	
2 tbsp	lemon juice	25 mL
1/4 cup	granulated sugar	50 mL
1 tbsp	rum (optional)	15 mL
	FILLING	
1/2 cup	granulated sugar	125 mL
1 tsp	grated lemon rind	5 mL
1/3 cup	lemon juice	75 mL
2 tbsp	butter	25 mL
2	eggs	2
1 cup	whipping cream	250 mL

Line 17- x 11-inch (45 x 29 cm) jelly roll pan with parchment or waxed paper. Grease paper and flour lightly. Set aside.

Combine hazelnuts, flour and lemon rind. In large bowl, beat egg yolks with 1/2 cup (125 mL) of the sugar for about 3 minutes or until thickened and pale yellow. Beat in vanilla. Gently fold in nut mixture.

With clean beaters and bowl, beat egg whites with cream of tartar until soft peaks form. Beat in remaining sugar until stiff peaks form. Stir one-quarter of the egg whites into yolk mixture. Fold in remaining egg whites.

Spread mixture evenly into prepared pan. Bake in 400°F (200°C) oven for 10 to 12 minutes or until cake springs back when pressed lightly in center. Let cool on rack.

LEMON SYRUP: Meanwhile, in small saucepan, bring lemon juice and sugar to boil; cook, stirring, until sugar dissolves. Stir in rum (if using). Let cool.

FILLING: In small nonaluminum saucepan, simmer sugar, lemon rind and juice and butter over medium heat, stirring, until sugar dissolves and butter melts.

In bowl, whisk eggs; gradually whisk in hot lemon mixture. Return to saucepan; cook over medium heat, stirring constantly, for about 1 minute or just until thickened. Strain into clean bowl; place plastic wrap directly on surface. Refrigerate for 30 minutes or until very cold. Whip cream; fold into lemon mixture.

To assemble, sprinkle icing sugar over cake. Loosen edges of cake and invert onto tea towel. Peel off paper. Trim any crusty edges. Sprinkle cake with syrup. Spread filling over top. Starting at short end, roll up cake. *(Roll can be frozen on baking sheet lined with plastic wrap or foil. Wrap frozen roll well with plastic wrap, then foil. To thaw, remove wrappings and place on serving platter in refrigerator for 5 hours.)*

Place cake on serving platter; dust lightly with icing sugar. Makes 10 to 12 servings.

TIP: Toast hazelnuts on baking sheet in 350°F (180°C) oven for about 10 minutes or until fragrant. Rub vigorously in tea towel to remove most of the brown skins. Finely chop or grind hazelnuts in food processor or blender.

Chocolate Brownie Turtle Cake

This decadent caramel brownie cake capitalizes on the flavor of the popular chocolate everyone loves.

4 oz	each semisweet and unsweetenedchocolate, chopped	125 g
3/4 cup	butter	175 mL
3	eggs	3
1-1/2 cups	granulated sugar	375 mL
1 tsp	vanilla	5 mL
3/4 cup	all-purpose flour	175 mL
3/4 tsp	baking powder	4 mL
Pinch	salt	Pinch
3/4 cup	chopped pecans	175 mL
3/4 cup	chocolate chips or chopped semisweet chocolate (optional)	175 mL
	CARAMEL LAYER	
10 oz	light caramels	300 g
2 tbsp	whipping cream	25 mL
	GLAZE	
6 oz	semisweet chocolate	175 g
1/3 cup	whipping cream	75 mL
	GARNISH	
12	pecan halves	12

In small bowl set over hot (not boiling) water, melt semi-sweet and unsweetened chocolate with butter; set aside. ❧ In large bowl, whisk together eggs, sugar and vanilla until well combined. Stir in chocolate mixture.

❧ Mix together flour, baking powder and salt; stir into chocolate mixture. Add pecans, and chocolate chips (if using), stirring just until combined.

❧ Scrape mixture into 9-inch (2.5 L) springform pan lined with parchment or waxed paper on bottom; bake in 350°F (180°C) oven for 45 minutes or just until cake starts to pull away from side and cracks on top. Let cool in pan on rack.

❧ CARAMEL LAYER: In small bowl set over saucepan of simmering water, melt caramels with cream, stirring occasionally, for 10 minutes or until smooth. Pour over brownie cake in pan. Refrigerate for 30 minutes or until set.

❧ GLAZE: In bowl set over hot (not boiling) water, melt chocolate with cream, whisking until smooth. Let cool slightly; pour over caramel layer. Garnish with pecans. Refrigerate for at least 4 hours or up to 24 hours. *(Cake can be wrapped well with plastic wrap in pan and frozen for up to 2 weeks; thaw in refrigerator for 5 hours.)*

❧ To serve, remove side of pan and transfer cake to serving platter; let stand at room temperature for 15 minutes. Makes 12 to 16 servings.

Marzipan

The food processor makes a simple job of homemade marzipan that's so good you'll find it hard to settle for the commercial variety again. Only freshly blanched, still-warm almonds will work.

2 cups	unblanched almonds (12 oz/375 g)	500 mL
2 cups	icing sugar	500 mL
2 tsp	almond extract	10 mL
2 tsp	corn syrup	10 mL
1	egg white, lightly beaten	1

In bowl, cover almonds with boiling water; let stand for 2 minutes. Drain and skin by firmly pressing one end to make nut pop through skin.

❧ In food processor, grind warm almonds for 1-1/2 to 2 minutes or until fine. Add icing sugar; mix for 1 minute or until blended, scraping down side of bowl when necessary. Blend in almond extract and corn syrup.

❧ With motor running, pour in enough of the egg white to form ball. Wrap in plastic wrap and place in plastic bag; refrigerate for at least 2 hours or until firm. Makes 1 lb (500 g) or 2 cups (500 mL).

Vanilla Wreaths

*Whether for eating or for decorating the tree, these
delicate cookie wreaths are a must for Christmas.*

1 cup	butter, softened	250 mL
1/2 cup	granulated sugar	125 mL
1/2 cup	marzipan (recipe, page 165)	125 mL
1 tbsp	vanilla	15 mL
1	egg	1
2 cups	all-purpose flour	500 mL

In large bowl, beat butter with sugar until fluffy; beat in marzipan, vanilla and egg until smooth. Gradually beat in flour until consistency of whipped cream.

❧ Using large piping bag with medium rosette tip, pipe 1-1/2-inch (4 cm) wreaths onto greased or parchment paper-lined baking sheets. Chill in refrigerator for 10 minutes.

❧ Bake in 375°F (190°C) oven for 10 to 12 minutes or until golden brown around edges. Let cool on pans. Makes about 84 cookies.

Finnish "Bread"

Crunchy almonds and coarse sugar add a festive appearance.

2-1/3 cups	all-purpose flour	575 mL
1/2 cup	granulated sugar	125 mL
1 cup	butter	250 mL
1	egg, beaten	1
1/4 cup	coarse sugar	50 mL
1/3 cup	finely chopped unblanched almonds	75 mL

In large bowl, stir together flour and granulated sugar; using pastry blender or two knives, cut in butter until in fine crumbs. Gather into ball; knead lightly until smooth and dough holds together.

❧ Divide dough into 6 portions. On lightly floured surface, roll each portion into 10-inch (25 cm) long log; flatten with knife to 1/2-inch (1 cm) thickness. Brush with egg; sprinkle with coarse sugar and almonds. Cut on diagonal into 1-inch (2.5 cm) wide slices to form diamond shapes.

❧ Bake on greased or parchment paper-lined baking sheets in 325°F (160°C) oven for 10 to 12 minutes or until golden brown on edges. Let cool on pans on rack for 5 minutes; remove to racks to let cool completely. *(Cookies can be frozen for up to 1 month.)* Makes about 54 cookies.

Invite friends and family for coffee and (clockwise from top) Finnish "Bread", King's Bread, Vanilla Wreaths and Spice Cookies.

King's Bread

This decadent, easy treat of marzipan coated with chocolate is more like candy than a cookie. Make your own marzipan or use a commercial one.

3 tbsp	raisins	50 mL
3 tbsp	dark rum	50 mL
1 cup	marzipan (8 oz/250 g) (see recipe, page 165)	250 mL
3 tbsp	mixed candied peel	50 mL
8 oz	bittersweet or semisweet chocolate, coarsely chopped	250 g
	Glazed cherries, halved	
	Walnut or pecan halves	

In small bowl, combine raisins and rum; cover and let stand overnight. Drain, reserving rum.

🍂 In bowl, break marzipan into small pieces; knead in candied peel and raisins until combined, adding reserved rum if too stiff. Form into two 1-inch (2.5 cm) diameter rolls. Wrap in plastic wrap; refrigerate for at least 4 hours or overnight.

🍂 Unwrap rolls and place on rack. In top of double boiler over hot (not boiling) water, melt chocolate; brush over rolls, turning to coat well all over. Press cherries and nuts along top of rolls.

🍂 Refrigerate rolls on rack for about 1 hour or until set. *(Rolls can be stored in refrigerator for up to 1 month.)* Let stand at room temperature for 10 minutes before cutting into 1/2-inch (1 cm) thick slices. Makes 20 slices.

TIP: A knife dipped in water makes slicing of these logs easier.

Spice Cookies

Similar to our gingerbread, these Danish Christmas cookies are usually rolled and cut in heart shapes, but you can use any Christmas cutters. Or, form dough into logs, ready to slice and bake when fresh cookies are needed.

1 cup	butter	250 mL
1 cup	granulated sugar	250 mL
1/2 cup	corn syrup	125 mL
2-3/4 cups	all-purpose flour	675 mL
1 cup	unblanched almonds, chopped	250 mL
1 tbsp	cinnamon	15 mL
2 tsp	ground ginger	10 mL
2 tsp	ground cloves	10 mL
1 tsp	baking soda	5 mL

In large bowl, beat butter with sugar until creamy; stir in corn syrup. Combine flour, almonds, cinnamon, ginger, cloves and baking soda; with wooden spoon, gradually stir into butter mixture to make soft, but not sticky, dough.

🍂 Divide dough into 4 portions. On lightly floured surface, roll each into 1-1/2-inch (4 cm) diameter log. Wrap in plastic wrap and refrigerate until chilled. *(Dough can be refrigerated overnight or frozen for up to 1 month; thaw before baking.)*

🍂 Cut rolls into 1/4-inch (5 mm) thick slices; place 1 inch (2.5 cm) apart on greased baking sheets. (Or, roll out dough between sheets of waxed paper; cut, using 2-inch/5 cm heart-shaped cookie cutter.)

🍂 Bake in 400°F (200°C) oven for 8 to 10 minutes or until golden brown. Let cool on pans for 3 minutes; remove to racks to let cool completely. Makes about 96 round or 72 heart cookies.

CANDLE MAGIC

Candles — symbols of light and joy — bring a feeling of warmth and welcome to your holiday decor. But smoking, dripping candles can ruin the setting. Here are some tips to light up your celebrations and make candles last.

🍃 There are two reasons candles smoke: either they're in a draft or the wick is too long. The ideal wick length is 1/2 inch (1 cm) above the wax. New candle wicks should be trimmed before they're burned.

🍃 If the flame is small, sputters and then goes out, the wick is too short. This can be remedied by digging the wick out to its proper length with a sharp knife.

🍃 Before using, chill candles in the refrigerator so they'll burn slowly and evenly.

🍃 Never blow a candle out. It causes smoking and hot wax to spatter. Instead, use a teaspoon or candle snuffer.

🍃 To look and perform their best, candles must be kept clean. A piece of nylon stocking is best for taking off dust and restoring luster. Before storing, wipe candle with alcohol, then store in a cool dark place.

NOUVELLE FEASTING IN QUEBEC
MENU

Vegetable Terrine with
Fresh Parsley Sauce*

Curried Apple Soup*

Maple-Glazed Roast Ducks with Turnip*

Wild Rice Pilaf*

Green Beans with Almonds

Cinnamon Ice Cream in Tulip Petal Cups*

Recipes included

Vegetable Terrine

Make this delectable terrine, a specialty of Dominique Guilbeault, the day before serving so it sets properly.
Unmould onto a serving platter, or slice and serve on individual plates with a spoonful of parsley sauce.

2	pkg (each 7 g) gelatin	2
4	large carrots (1 lb/500 g), sliced	4
1/2 tsp	dried dillweed	2 mL
3/4 tsp	each salt and pepper	4 mL
1 cup	light mayonnaise	250 mL
1	pkg (10 oz/284 g) fresh spinach	1
2 tbsp	lemon juice	25 mL
Pinch	cayenne pepper	Pinch
4	large parsnips (1 lb/500 g), peeled and sliced	4
1/4 tsp	ground nutmeg	1 mL
	Fresh Parsley Sauce (see recipe, below)	

In small saucepan, combine gelatin with 1/2 cup (125 mL) water; let stand for about 10 minutes or until softened. Cook over low heat, stirring, until gelatin has dissolved. Remove from heat; set aside.

In heavy saucepan, pour in enough cold water to just cover carrots; cover and bring to boil. Boil for 15 minutes or until very tender and water has evaporated.

In food processor, purée carrots until smooth. Add dill, 1/4 tsp (1 mL) each of the salt and pepper, 1/3 cup (75 mL) of the mayonnaise and 3 tbsp (50 mL) of the gelatin mixture; combine until smooth. Spoon into 8- x 4-inch (1.5 L) plastic wrap-lined loaf pan; refrigerate.

Trim and rinse spinach under cold running water; shake off excess. In heavy saucepan, cook spinach, with just the water clinging to leaves, for about 5 minutes or just until wilted. Drain and squeeze dry.

In food processor, purée spinach. Add 1/4 tsp (1 mL) each of the salt and pepper, 1/3 cup (75 mL) of the mayonnaise, 2 tbsp (25 mL) of the gelatin mixture, lemon juice and cayenne; combine until smooth. Spread over carrot layer; refrigerate.

In heavy saucepan, pour in enough cold water to cover parsnips; cover and bring to boil. Cook for about 15 minutes or until very tender and water has evaporated.

In food processor, purée parsnips until smooth. Add remaining salt and pepper, mayonnaise, gelatin mixture and nutmeg; combine until smooth. Spread over spinach layer. Cover and refrigerate for at least 8 hours or until chilled and set. *(Terrine can be refrigerated for up to 2 days.)* Serve with Fresh Parsley Sauce. Makes 8 servings.

Fresh Parsley Sauce

Quick to make at the last minute, or make the day before,
this simple uncooked sauce is also delicious with fish or cold chicken.

1 cup	loosely packed parsley leaves	250 mL
1/3 cup	vegetable oil	75 mL
2 tbsp	lemon juice	25 mL
1-1/2 tsp	Dijon mustard	7 mL
1/4 tsp	each salt and pepper	1 mL

In food processor, chop parsley. Combine oil, lemon juice, mustard, salt and pepper. With motor running, pour in oil mixture; process until well combined. Cover and refrigerate for up to 1 day. Makes 1/2 cup (125 mL).

Wild Rice Pilaf

*Truly Canadian, wild rice is a treat and a fine accompaniment
to roast duck — or turkey. You can purchase fines herbes, a mixture of dried herbs
(usually chervil, chives, parsley and tarragon), at specialty food stores.*

1 cup	wild rice	250 mL
2 tbsp	butter	25 mL
1	large onion, finely chopped	1
2	duck livers, chopped (optional)	2
3/4 cup	cooked chestnuts, coarsely chopped	175 mL
1/2 cup	sultana raisins	125 mL
2 tbsp	fines herbes	25 mL
Pinch	ground nutmeg	Pinch
3 cups	chicken stock	750 mL
1 cup	long grain white rice	250 mL
	Salt and pepper	
1/2 cup	chopped fresh parsley	125 mL

In small bowl, cover wild rice with cold water; soak for 1-1/2 hours. Drain well and set aside.

In large heavy saucepan, melt butter over medium heat; cook onion, stirring, for 2 minutes. Add duck livers (if using); cook for 1 minute. Stir in wild rice, chestnuts, raisins, fines herbes and nutmeg; cook, stirring, for 2 minutes.

Stir in stock; cover and bring to boil. Reduce heat to medium-low; simmer, covered, for 20 minutes.

Stir in white rice; cook, covered, for 20 minutes or until rice is tender and liquid is absorbed. Season with salt and pepper to taste. *(Pilaf can be refrigerated in airtight container. To reheat, transfer to covered casserole; sprinkle with 1/2 cup/125 mL water. Bake in 350°F/180°C oven for 20 minutes.)* Sprinkle with parsley. Makes 8 servings.

Maple-Glazed Roast Ducks with Turnip

*Quebeckers, proud of their fresh seasonal local food, often opt for a change of pace
from the traditional turkey of Christmas. Complemented by a maple glaze, these succulent ducks will update
a holiday meal. You can use rutabagas instead of turnips if you like.*

2	ducks (each 6-1/2 lb/3 kg)	2
	Salt and pepper	
2 cups	chicken stock	500 mL
1/2 cup	maple syrup	125 mL
8	small turnips, peeled	8

Remove giblets and necks from ducks. Rinse ducks inside and out under cold water; pat dry. Trim fat from both ends. Sprinkle each cavity lightly with salt and pepper. Truss ducks at both ends with poultry pins or skewers. Tuck wing tips behind back. Pierce through skin only with fork, without piercing flesh.

Place ducks, breast side up, on rack in large roasting pan. Roast in 400°F (200°C) oven for 20 minutes. Cover breasts with foil, dull side out, leaving legs and thighs exposed. Reduce heat to 350°F (180°C); bake for 1 hour and 45 minutes or until meat thermometer inserted in thigh registers 180°F (80°C). Transfer ducks to baking sheet; keep warm.

Skim off fat in roasting pan. Stir in stock and bring to boil, stirring to scrape up brown bits; cook over medium-high heat for 5 to 10 minutes or until reduced to 1 cup (250 mL). Add maple syrup; cook for 3 to 5 minutes or until slightly thickened. Remove glaze and set aside.

Return ducks to pan and brush with about 1/4 cup (50 mL) of the glaze; bake for 5 minutes. Brush with another 1/4 cup (50 mL) of the glaze; bake for 20 minutes. Transfer to cutting board and tent with foil; let stand for 20 minutes.

Meanwhile, in saucepan, pour in enough cold water to just cover turnips; bring to boil. Reduce heat and simmer for 20 minutes or just until tender; drain and set aside.

Pour remaining glaze into saucepan; bring to boil. Reduce heat and add cooked turnips; simmer for about 12 minutes or until warmed through and evenly coated. Serve with ducks. Makes 8 servings.

Curried Apple Soup

A subtle hint of curry balances the sweetness of the apples in this smooth, creamy soup. A thin slice of unpeeled apple makes a nice garnish.

1 tbsp	butter	15 mL
2	stalks celery, finely chopped	2
Half	large onion, finely chopped	Half
2 tsp	curry powder	10 mL
8	apples, peeled and sliced	8
4 cups	chicken stock	1 L
Pinch	each cinnamon and ground nutmeg	Pinch
1/2 cup	whipping cream	125 mL
	Salt and pepper	

In large saucepan, melt butter over medium heat; cook celery and onion, stirring occasionally, for 10 minutes or until softened but not browned. Stir in curry powder; cook, stirring constantly, for 1 minute.

🍂 Add apples, stock, cinnamon and nutmeg; cover and simmer for 25 minutes or until apples are very soft.

🍂 In blender, purée soup, in batches. Return to saucepan; stir in cream. Season with salt and pepper to taste. Heat through. Makes 8 servings.

TIP: If the soup is too thick, stir in a little water.

MULLED RED WINE

Greet your guests with a warm glass of mulled red wine. Choose a modest house wine for the base. Any leftovers can be refrigerated for up to two weeks.

🍂 In large pot over medium heat, heat 3 bottles (each 1 L) red wine, 1/2 cup (125 mL) granulated sugar, 4 sliced oranges, 4 sliced lemons, 8 cinnamon sticks and 15 whole cloves to just below boiling. Simmer for 30 minutes. Serve warm. Makes 8 servings.

— 173 —

Cinnamon Ice Cream

This creamy, aromatic ice cream makes a special ending to a meal, especially when served in dainty Tulip Petal Cups (recipe, below).

6	egg yolks	6
2/3 cup	granulated sugar	150 mL
2 cups	whipping cream	500 mL
1 cup	light cream	250 mL
2 tsp	cinnamon	10 mL

In large bowl, whisk together egg yolks and sugar for about 2 minutes or until pale and thickened.

❧ Meanwhile, in heavy saucepan, heat 1 cup (250 mL) of the whipping cream and light cream just until tiny bubbles form around edge of pan. Gradually pour into yolk mixture, whisking constantly; whisk in cinnamon.

❧ Transfer mixture to saucepan; cook over low heat, stirring constantly, for 5 to 8 minutes or until custard is thick enough to coat back of spoon. Do not boil. Immediately strain into bowl; stir in remaining whipping cream. Let cool to room temperature; cover with plastic wrap and refrigerate for at least 2 hours or until chilled. (*Custard can be refrigerated for up to 24 hours.*)

❧ Freeze in ice-cream maker according to manufacturer's instructions. (Or, transfer to metal pan; freeze for 4 hours or until almost firm. Break up into chunks and transfer to food processor; purée until smooth. Pour into chilled airtight container; freeze for 1 hour or until firm.) Freeze for up to 2 days. Transfer to refrigerator 30 minutes before serving. Makes about 4 cups (1 L), or 8 servings.

Tulip Petal Cups

Delicious with any flavor of ice cream or sorbet, these cups can be made ahead. Be sure to handle with care.

1/3 cup	butter, softened	75 mL
2/3 cup	granulated sugar	150 mL
1 cup	all-purpose flour	250 mL
3	egg whites, lightly beaten	3
1 tsp	almond extract	5 mL

In bowl, beat butter with sugar at medium speed for 2 minutes or until fluffy. Using wooden spoon, stir in flour, in two additions, until mixture is crumbly. Stir in egg whites, 1 tbsp (15 mL) at a time, stirring until creamy. Stir in almond extract.

❧ On half of well-greased baking sheet, drop 2 tbsp (25 mL) of the batter. Spread with spatula or back of spoon to form 5-1/2-inch (13 cm) circle. Repeat on other half of sheet.

❧ Bake in 400°F (200°C) oven for 6 to 8 minutes or just until golden brown at edges. Working quickly, remove baking sheet from oven, place on rack and immediately slide palette knife under cookies. Place into 4-1/4-inch (11 cm) diameter bowls.

❧ Gently press each cookie into bowl with 2-1/2-inch (6 cm) diameter glass, to form tulip shape. Let baking sheet cool; wipe clean with paper towel and grease again. Repeat with remaining batter. (*Cups can be stored in airtight container for up to 3 days.*) Makes 12 cookie cups.

TIP: When making the cookie cups, work quickly to avoid cooling, which can cause the cookies to crack.

Potato Latkes

Lacy, golden latkes — crisp potato pancakes — are a special Jewish dish at Hannukah festivities.
But these easy-to-make pancakes, delicious with applesauce and sour cream, are easy to eat all year round.

5	baking potatoes (2-1/2 lb/1.25 kg)	5
2	small onions, quartered	2
3	eggs	3
3 tbsp	all-purpose flour	50 mL
3/4 tsp	salt	4 mL
1/4 tsp	pepper	1 mL
	Vegetable oil for cooking	
	Sour cream and/or applesauce	

Peel potatoes. By hand, or in food processor using shredder blade, alternately shred onion quarters and potatoes. Transfer to colander. With hands, squeeze out as much moisture as possible, discarding liquid. Transfer to large bowl. Mix in eggs, flour, salt and pepper; let stand for 5 minutes. Pour off any liquid.

❧ In large skillet, heat 1/4 inch (5 mm) oil over high heat until hot but not smoking. Add 1/4 cup (50 mL) mixture per latke, leaving about 1 inch (2.5 cm) between each; flatten slightly with back of spoon. Fry for 3 minutes or until well browned and crisp around edges. With slotted spatula, turn and fry for 2 to 3 minutes longer or until crisp and golden brown.

❧ Transfer to paper towels; drain well. Repeat with remaining mixture, removing any cooked bits from skillet and adding more oil as necessary. *(Latkes can be frozen for up to 2 weeks. Partially thaw and reheat in 450°F/230°C oven for 5 to 8 minutes.)* Serve immediately with sour cream or applesauce. Makes about 22 latkes, or 4 to 6 servings.

VARIATIONS

❧ SAGE AND PARSLEY LATKES: Add 1/2 tsp (2 mL) dried sage and 1/2 cup (125 mL) chopped fresh parsley to batter along with eggs.

❧ CARROT LATKES: Substitute 1 cup (250 mL) grated carrots (about 4) for 1 of the potatoes. Add to shredded potato and onion mixture.

HOLIDAY TRADITIONS

Here's a sampling of the rich and diverse holiday traditions celebrated throughout Canada during this time of year.

❧ Jewish families celebrate Hannukah, often called the Festival of Lights. This celebration, which revolves around the lighting of candles, one each night for eight days, falls in November or December. Holiday foods such as potato pancakes, called latkes (recipe above), are served with applesauce and sour cream.

❧ Scandinavian families celebrate their festival of lights, St. Lucia Day, on December 13. For a special breakfast treat that day, they serve golden, saffron buns.

❧ The Portuguese in Canada celebrate Christmas Day (Dia da Familia) with church services and family gatherings. Bolo Rei (King's Cake) is their traditional bread filled with candied fruit and spirits. At the stroke of midnight on Passagem do Ano (the beginning of the new year), they eat 12 raisins for good luck, one with each stroke of the clock.

❧ Ukrainians and many others from Eastern Orthodox churches follow the Julian calendar and celebrate Christmas on January 7. Their special "holy supper" consists of 12 meatless and milkless dishes, often including borscht (beet soup), cabbage rolls and pyrohy (dumplings).

❧ Other Canadians carry out heritage traditions during the Christmas and New Year's season. Greeks and Macedonians eat special cakes with a coin baked inside. Italians feast on a meatless Christmas Eve dinner; their Christmas bread is a rich panettone. German-Canadians favor roast goose and dumplings and red cabbage. And all Scots love round cakes of buttery shortbread.

❧ The Chinese celebrate a glorious New Year's tradition that becomes a big birthday party for everyone. As many family members as possible gather to bid farewell to the old year and welcome the new. The dinner table, set with a red cloth and red candles, offers 12 vegetarian dishes — one for each year in the zodiac. Lichee nuts, oranges and kumquats are favorite gifts for visitors, while small red envelopes holding money are given to the children.

CHRISTMAS TEA
MENU

Savory Cheddar Cheesecake* | Mince Tarts and Shortbread

Cranberry Orange Chutney* | Assorted Cookies

Cheese Scones* | Hot Tea
or Cranberry Tea Punch*

Party Sandwiches

Chocolate Fingers* | *Recipes included

Savory Cheddar Cheesecake

This cheese spread has wonderful aged Cheddar flavor with a hint of orange and spice.
Serve with whole wheat crackers and fresh fruit. It's delicious topped with Cranberry Orange Chutney.

1 lb	orange old Cheddar cheese, shredded	500 g
1	pkg (250 g) cream cheese	1
1/2 cup	butter, softened	125 mL
1 tsp	grated orange rind	5 mL
2 tbsp	orange juice	25 mL
1 tbsp	Dijon mustard	15 mL
1/4 tsp	ground nutmeg	1 mL

In food processor, blend together Cheddar cheese, cream cheese and butter until combined. Add orange rind and juice, mustard and nutmeg; blend just until thick and creamy.

❧ Spoon into 8-inch (2 L) plastic wrap-lined springform pan, smoothing top. Cover and refrigerate for at least 8 hours or until chilled and firm. *(Cheesecake can be refrigerated for up to 3 days.)*

❧ To serve, remove side of pan; peel off plastic wrap. Transfer to serving plate; let stand for 30 minutes. Makes 16 servings.

Cranberry Orange Chutney

Full of cranberries, raisins and currants, this chutney pairs up well with the Christmas turkey or ham.

3 cups	fresh cranberries	750 mL
1 cup	chopped onions	250 mL
1 cup	each raisins and currants	250 mL
1 cup	cider vinegar	250 mL
3/4 cup	each granulated and packed brown sugar	175 mL
1 tbsp	grated orange rind	15 mL
1/2 cup	orange juice	125 mL
1 tsp	each salt, cinnamon, ground cloves and ginger	5 mL

In large saucepan, stir together cranberries, onions, raisins, currants, vinegar, granulated and brown sugars, orange rind and juice, salt, cinnamon, cloves and ginger; bring to boil. Reduce heat to medium-low; simmer, stirring often, for 20 minutes or until thickened.

❧ Ladle into hot, sterilized canning jars, leaving 1/2-inch (1 cm) headspace; seal and refrigerate for up to 2 weeks. (For longer storage, process in boiling water bath for 5 minutes.) Makes about 5 cups (1.25 L).

Cranberry Tea Punch

Pink and fizzy, this cinnamon-flavored decaffeinated tea punch is great for kids and adults alike.
As an extra treat, add a spoonful of lemon or lime sherbet to each child's glass.

3	decaffeinated tea bags	3
1	stick cinnamon	1
2	cans (each 275 mL) frozen Cranberry Cocktail concentrate, thawed	2
1	can (12 oz/375 mL) ginger ale	1
	Lime slices	
	Ice cubes	

In teapot, pour 3 cups (750 mL) boiling water over tea bags and cinnamon stick; let steep for 5 minutes. Remove tea bags and cinnamon; let cool.

❧ Pour into punch bowl along with Cranberry Cocktail concentrate and 2-1/2 cups (625 mL) water; refrigerate until chilled.

❧ Just before serving, stir in ginger ale; float lime slices and ice cubes on top. Makes 9 cups (2.25 L).

Chocolate Fingers

These easy no-bake bars are mocha flavored, glazed with chocolate, then chilled until set.
They keep for several days refrigerated, provided they are well hidden!

1	pkg (400 g) digestive biscuits	1
1/2 cup	finely chopped nuts	125 mL
1/2 cup	butter	125 mL
1/2 cup	granulated sugar	125 mL
1/2 cup	sifted unsweetened cocoa powder	125 mL
1 tbsp	instant coffee granules	15 mL
1 tbsp	hot water	15 mL
2	eggs, beaten	2
2 tsp	vanilla	10 mL
	CHOCOLATE GLAZE	
1 cup	semisweet chocolate chips	250 mL
2 tbsp	shortening	25 mL

In food processor or with rolling pin, crush biscuits until in fine crumbs. Transfer to bowl and add nuts.

In top of double boiler or bowl set over simmering water, melt butter; whisk in sugar and cocoa. Dissolve coffee in hot water; add to pan and cook, whisking, for 1 minute or until thickened and sugar has dissolved.

Whisk in eggs and vanilla; cook, whisking, for 4 to 5 minutes or until thickened slightly. Remove from heat; with fork, stir in crumb mixture. Pack into waxed or parchment paper-lined 8-inch (2 L) square cake pan. Cover and refrigerate for about 1 hour or until cool.

CHOCOLATE GLAZE: In top of double boiler, stir chocolate with shortening until melted. Pour over base, spreading evenly and making design with fork. Cover and refrigerate until set. Using paper as handles, lift square from pan. Cut into fingers. Makes 28 fingers.

Cheese Scones

Light as air and flecked with cheese, these scones can be split and spread lightly with softened butter and
your favorite chutney. Top with thin slices of chicken or shaved smoked ham or turkey.

2-1/2 cups	all-purpose flour	625 mL
1 tbsp	each baking powder and granulated sugar	15 mL
1 tsp	baking soda	5 mL
1/2 tsp	salt	2 mL
1/2 tsp	dried thyme (optional)	2 mL
3/4 cup	butter	175 mL
1 cup	shredded old Cheddar cheese	250 mL
1/2 cup	plain yogurt	125 mL
1/2 cup	(approx) milk	125 mL

In large bowl, combine flour, baking powder, sugar, baking soda, salt, and thyme (if using). With pastry blender or two knives, cut in butter until crumbly. Stir in Cheddar cheese. Add yogurt and milk all at once, stirring with fork to make slightly sticky dough.

Turn out dough onto lightly floured surface; knead gently 6 times or until smooth. Pat into rectangle about 1/2 inch (1 cm) thick.

With 1-1/2-inch (4 cm) round cookie cutter, cut out rounds; place on greased baking sheet and brush with milk. Bake in 450°F (230°C) oven for 10 to 12 minutes or until lightly browned. Makes 36 scones.

Cranberry Conserve

Here's a rich, fruit-packed Christmas conserve that's easy to make, easy on the budget and easy to enjoy.

3 cups	fresh cranberries	750 mL
3	seedless oranges (unpeeled), finely chopped	3
1	can (14 oz/398 mL) crushed pineapple (undrained)	1
3/4 cup	dried apricots, finely chopped	175 mL
1	pkg (57 g) regular fruit pectin crystals	1
5 cups	granulated sugar	1.25 L

In saucepan, combine cranberries, oranges and pineapple, crushing some of the cranberries with potato masher; cook over medium heat for 15 minutes.

Stir in apricots and pectin crystals; bring to full rolling boil over high heat. Stir in sugar. Return to full rolling boil over high heat; boil for 1-1/2 minutes. Remove from heat; stir and skim off foam.

Ladle into hot sterilized canning jars, leaving 1/4-inch (5 mm) headspace. Seal and process in boiling water bath for 5 minutes. Makes 8 cups (2 L).

Toffee Cookie Brittle

Packed with chocolate chips and milk chocolate-covered toffee, these winners have the novel twist of being broken into irregular shapes.

1-1/4 cups	butter, softened	300 mL
1-1/2 cups	granulated sugar	375 mL
1-1/2 tsp	vanilla	7 mL
1/2 tsp	salt	2 mL
3 cups	all-purpose flour	750 mL
1 cup	chocolate chips	250 mL
6	bars (each 39 g) milk chocolate-covered toffee, chopped	6

In bowl, beat butter with sugar until light and fluffy; beat in vanilla and salt. With wooden spoon, gradually stir in flour until combined. Stir in chocolate chips and chopped candy bars.

Gently squeeze handfuls of dough just until mixture holds together; pat evenly into ungreased 17- x 11-inch (45 x 29 cm) jelly roll pan. Bake in 325°F (160°C) oven for about 30 minutes or until just firm to the touch. Let cool in pan on rack; break into pieces. Makes about 60 pieces.

Fat-Cat Truffles

Kids and grown-ups alike enjoy finding several of these on a tray of sweet treats.

2 oz	semisweet chocolate	60 g
1/3 cup	light rum or orange juice	75 mL
1/4 cup	icing sugar	50 mL
1/4 cup	corn syrup	50 mL
2 cups	finely crushed vanilla wafer crumbs	500 mL
1 cup	finely ground almonds	250 mL
	DECORATION	
4 oz	semisweet chocolate, melted	120 g
	Toasted sliced almonds	
	Coconut	
	Red or black shoestring licorice	

In top of double boiler over hot (not boiling) water, melt chocolate. Remove from heat; stir in rum, icing sugar and corn syrup.

Combine wafer crumbs and ground almonds; stir into chocolate mixture, blending well. Refrigerate for 30 minutes or until firm enough to shape into 1-1/2 inch (4 cm) balls.

DECORATION: Coat truffles with melted chocolate. Attach almond slices for ears, bits of almonds for eyes, coconut for whiskers and licorice for tails. Let stand on waxed paper-lined baking sheet until set. Makes 24 truffles.

Cranberry Conserve

The Contributors

For your easy reference, we have included a listing of material by contributor — organized alphabetically, with a page reference.

Claire Arfin
Thai-Style Chicken, 52

Julian Armstrong and Dominique Guilbeault
Cinnamon Ice Cream in Tulip Petal Cups, 174
Curried Apple Soup, 173
Maple-Glazed Roast Ducks with Turnip, 172
Vegetable Terrine, 171
Wild Rice Pilaf, 172

Carla Azevedo
Christmas Fig Cake, 160
Panpepato, 160

Elizabeth Baird
Cocktail Patties, 20
Concord Grape Pie with Orange Pastry, 142
Crispy Fish Cakes, 55
Georgian Bay Apple Pie, 140
Ginger Cake, 28
Harvest Pumpkin Pie, 138
Jerk Roast Pork, 19
Nutty Coleslaw, 20
Quick Hot Cross Buns, 88
Rice and "Peas", 19
Oven-Roasted Parsnips, 17

Spinach and Strawberry Salad, 92
Summer Harvest Chicken Salad, 119
Warm Lamb Salad, 119
White Wine and Green Grape Sangria, 143

Emily Bright
Spicy Apple Drink, 151

James Chatto
Orange Pork Chops, 63
Saucy Seasoned Sole, 21

Janet Cornish
Mini Meat Loaf Muffins, 56

Ellen Cornwall
Pan Bagnat, 114

Bonnie Cowan
Sesame Chicken with Asparagus, 94

Nancy Enright
Croque-Monsieur, 71
Old-Fashioned Chocolate Shake, 80
Orange-Glazed Chicken Wings, 72
Peppers Stuffed with Rice, Corn and Tomatoes, 135
Veggie Platter with Dip, 72

Louise Faucher
Quebec Maple Syrup Pie, 96

Carol Ferguson
Chocolate Chip Cookies, 78
Chocolate Chip Hermits, 145

Margaret Fraser
Couscous Pilaf Salad, 116
Fat-Cat Truffles, 182
Frozen Banana Pops, 80
Shepherd's Pie with Three Peppers, 56

Barb Holland
Chicken Fajitas, 53
Lamb Moussaka, 13
Microwave Beef-Topped Tostadas, 59
Microwave Lemon-Herb Chicken and Vegetables, 52
Microwave Savory Onion and Cheese Bake, 67

Heather Howe
Pancake ABCs, 77
Quick Whole Wheat Pizza, 65

Marion Kane
Hoisin Ribs, 62

Kathryn Lamb
The Little Hatters' Tea Party, 48

Anne Lindsay
Cheese and Pepperoni Pizza, 71
Greek Salad Sandwiches, 123

Green Vegetable Risotto, 66
Grilled Chicken Breast with Fruit Salsa Sandwich, 123
Meatball and Penne Casserole, 15
Mediterranean Vegetable Stew, 67
Pot Roast with Onions, 14
Quick-Mixing Pizza Dough, 68
Rutabaga and Pear Purée, 136
Smoked Turkey with Asparagus Sandwich, 123
Stuffed Sherried Chicken Breasts, 12
Vegetable Burritos, 75

Birthe Marie Macdonald
Finnish "Bread", 166
King's Bread, 168
Marzipan, 165
Spice Cookies, 168
Vanilla Wreaths, 166

Jan Main
Banana Bran Carrot Mini Muffins, 79
Cheese Scones, 181
Chocolate Fingers, 181
Cranberry Orange Chutney, 180
Cranberry Tea Punch, 180
Jelly Belly, 80
Power Drink, 80
Savory Cheddar Cheesecake, 180

Photography Credits

SERGE BEAUCHEMIN: pages 48 and 49.

FRED BIRD: front cover; pages 12, 15, 16, 18, 21, 22, 26, 38, 40, 43, 44, 50, 54, 55, 57, 58, 62, 63, 64, 66, 68, 69, 70, 79, 82 and 83, 86, 89, 91, 92, 95, 97, 98, 99 (top), 100, 103, 115, 116, 120 and 121, 123, 126, 128, 135, 139, 142, 144, 152 and 153, 154, 161, 162, 173, 176, 183.

PETER BOLLI: page 99 (bottom).

CHRISTOPHER CAMPBELL: pages 35, 36 (bottom), 76, 77, 81, 104, 107, 108, 125, 148.

DAN COUTO: page 150.

DAVE FIELD: page 131.

MIKE GLUSS: page 137 (left).

FRANK GRANT: pages 1, 2 and 3, 5, 8 and 9, 34, 36 (top), 37, 73, 74, 90, 113, 130, 132, 141.

CHRISTOPHER LAWSON: page 149.

MICHAEL LEE: page 146 (left).

MICHAEL MAHOVLICH: page 25.

MARK MAINGUY: pages 178 and 179.

BROCK MAY: pages 137 (top right), 146 (inset).

KAREN PERLMUTTER: page 89 (inset).

JOHN STEPHENS: pages 32 and 33, 93, 169.

PETER H. STRANKS: pages 110, 112.

MIKE VISSER: pages 31, 88.

MICHAEL WARING: pages 10, 29, 60, 147.

ROBERT WIGINGTON: pages 158, 167, 170, 175.

MATTHEW WILEY: page 39.

Special thanks to Katherine O'Donnell and her parents for sharing her Little Hatter's Birthday Tea Party with us (photograph, pages 48 and 49) — along with friends Mellissa Nash, Lisa Demers, Britain Kendall, Halley Smith, Amanda Demers, Dominique Dery and Katherine's brother, James.

Index

Canadian Living's Family Cookbook

EDITORIAL DIRECTOR: Hugh Brewster

PROJECT EDITOR: Carol Sherman

SUPERVISING EDITOR: Wanda Nowakowska

EDITORIAL ASSISTANCE: Beverley Renahan

PRODUCTION DIRECTOR: Susan Barrable

PRODUCTION COORDINATOR: Donna Chong

BOOK DESIGN AND LAYOUT: Gordon Sibley Design Inc.

COLOR SEPARATION: Colour Technologies

PRINTING AND BINDING: Friesen Printers

CANADIAN LIVING ADVISORY BOARD:
Elizabeth Baird, Bonnie Baker Cowan, Anna Hobbs,
Caren King, Greg MacNeil

CANADIAN LIVING'S™ FAMILY COOKBOOK
was produced for The Quantum Book Group Inc.
by Madison Press Books